ITALIAN
COOKING

ITALIAN COOKING

John Varnom

CHARTWELL
BOOKS, INC.

DEDICATION

Questo libro è dedicato alla Signora Olga Bernardi di
Capanna Kind a Sportinia, senza la quale non avrei potuto
scrivere una sola parola. Ti ringrazio, Olga.

Ringrazio, anche il mio fratello Raisa Giorgio, cuoco
straordinario, Salvatore, campione di scacchi, e tutti i
personali di Capanna Kind: Olgina, Michele, Italo, Claudia,
Pipo, Franco Allemand e Bruno Capelli.

Thanks also to Daphne Page and Kevin Rourke for their
friendship and guidance, and Deirdre Slevin for her good
humor.

Und endlich Helga Röhrs, mein echter Schatz, für alles.

Published in 2003 by Chartwell Books
A Division of Book Sales, Inc.
114 Northfield Avenue
Edison, New Jersey 08837

This edition produced for sale in the U.S.A., its
territories, and dependencies only.

A QUINTET BOOK

ISBN 0-7858-1729-8

This book was designed and produced by
Quintet Publishing Limited
6 Blundell Street
London N7 9BH

Art Director: Peter Bridgewater
Designers: Ian Hunt, Martin Vincent
Editors: Shaun Barrington, Caroline Beattie
Susie Ward
Photographer: Trevor Wood
Food Preparation and Styling:
Jonathan Higgings, Judith Kelsey

Typeset in Great Britain by
Central Southern Typesetters, Eastbourne
Manufactured in Hong Kong by
Regent Publishing Services
Printed in Singapore by
Star Standard Industries (Pte) Ltd.

Contents

Introduction

First, let me state what is obvious to anyone with a well-balanced personality, flawless taste, and a proper experience of Italian knife and fork work: Italian food is better than French. We can support this proposition with a quote if we have to: "The Chinese taught the Italians to cook and the Italians taught the French." That this old saying is also a near-granite foundation stone in the dizzy edifice of gastronomic cliché need not trouble us. It happens to be true, for does not history relate how Marco Polo brought noodles and a few other things back to Venice from China and how some time later Catherine de Medici sent her chefs to the court of the Sun King to cook supper for that gang?

However, you, in your polite liberal way, may feel it is invidious to rank national cuisines in this manner. In that case, the next time you find yourself strolling an Icelandic beach, tread carefully, or you might fall into their national dish. That confection entails the burying of a superbly fresh whole cod in the sand, until flesh, bones, and innards run together in a kind of viscous ooze. Preparation time three months, oven temperature anything below zero. Participants at the feast then despatch their portions as quickly as possible with the aid of firewater, concerning which each man agrees to drink at least twice as much as he can hold. The dessert menu is unclear, although it is probably something palate-cleansing involving lichen and raw glacier.

Stil undecided? Then try eating, in turn, at each of the first ten restaurants, pubs, or cafés you encounter on a drive through any part of the English countryside. Suddenly, the frigid seas of Iceland, its rocky shores, the gun-metal gleam of its ancient ice-fields, may seem strangely welcoming.

Back to Italy, however, truly a paradise on earth for anyone but an Italian filling in a ricevuta fiscale or trying to organize the paperwork for a divorce. Why is Italian food so magnificent? And what is a trattoria?

The trattoria – pronounced, by the way, like "mamma mia" with the stress on the final "i" – is more or less the Italian equivalent of a bistro. Trattorie are supposed to be simple places, and the clearest sign that you are in

Left Amalfi, the first Italian maritime republic, has a history stretching back to the 6th century AD. It is famous for its fish restaurants and delicacies.

Left Capri, the island in the Bay of Naples where the Emperor Tiberius held his notorious orgies and the Bay of Naples itself, seen from above Sorrento (**right**). Naples, famous for its pizza, is the gastronomic capital of the south.

one will be the absence of a menu. They are also, strictly speaking, family run.

Of course, strict speaking is scarcely anything to rely on in these anarchic times. Have we not all visited "trattori" as big as Mussolini's railway stations, swarming with men in monkey suits brandishing gold-tasseled menus, in which twenty ways of sacrificing veal are lovingly described? In such cases, "trattoria" is simply thought to be a friendlier way of saying "ristorante."

In real-life trattorie, the dishes of the day – a soup maybe, a couple of pastas probably, and three or four main courses – will be described to you in person by whoever takes your order. A wine list would be unusual. And as for those things they shove round on wheels, groaning with out-of-season strawberries, half-a-dozen mass-produced gateaux, and oranges in caramel, forget it.

In short, a true trattoria will not attempt to offer its customers an extended pre-set menu or list of wines. On offer will be what the chef has decided to cook that day, and there is no guarantee that his or her ideas will conform to the titles found in cookery books. But what can you expect, from spaghetti bolognese?

Perhaps not even that. Bologna, the city from which the sauce takes its name, is the culinary capital of all that is rich in Italian cooking and even the Bolognese think almost twice before serving meat with pasta. Spaghetti bolognese, and the twenty kinds of veal, are items found just about exclusively outside Italy.

From a technical point of view, there is something else found exclusively outside Italy, and its astonishing rarity on home territory gives us a big clue to the true nature of the Italian kitchen. This item is sauces in general. The Italians do make besciamella. And there are a thousand sughi for the extraordinary range of pasta available. But there are no sauces in the French sense.

The Italians consider the real basics are the ingredients themselves. Each will have its own merit. The task of the chef is to identify that merit, and then tease it out by sympathetic treatment. This frequently means that the actual cooking process is an excessively simple one and, in that respect, I think this book may surprise you a little. The cooking is very much the final touch. Artfully concealed by the dish's very simplicity is the intricate and delicate process by which the combination of ingredients is chosen, and its proportions agreed upon. This happens long before work in the kitchen begins. The requisites are quality and freshness, neither of which need have anything whatever to do with expense.

The one exception to what seems to be a genuine rule of simplicity appears to be pasta. In fact, what the Italians have done here is very clever. Whereas many cuisines serve some form of carbohydrate with the main dish as a kind of bulking agent, the Italians have removed it and elevated it to a course in its own right. This is the role of risotto, pasta, or polenta as starters, their proper place in the Italian scheme of things.

Potatoes, for example, are made into gnocchi and served smothered in Gorgonzola at the beginning. Or the rice is cooked with the ink and the flesh of inkfish and served in a perfumed and glistening black mound. Noodles come with fresh basil and pine nuts, or white truffles, or ceps, or are thinned into spaghetti and served with clams, or garlic and chili, or tomato and oregano. Once again, the Italians have separated out what other cultures seek to mingle and dealt with each item in a manner appropriate to itself. The flavors are left intact and the portions kept small.

Two things distinguish this separation process. One is the flawless taste we mentioned earlier. The other is Italy's own abundance of miraculous things to eat, an abundance not common to many other countries. But this need not deter anyone: to cook the food in this book, you have only to do some proper shopping.

So skim through the recipes and then set out for the best market, or supermarket, you know. Buy the freshest ingredients you can afford. Then go home and be kind to them, according to the instructions.

Top Outside Florence in the evening, the time of day all Florentines settle down to their evening meal. Florentines eat well but simply, disdaining the complicated sauces and seasonings of other regions. **Right** The harbour at Sorrento, where fish fresh from the sea is the local specialty.

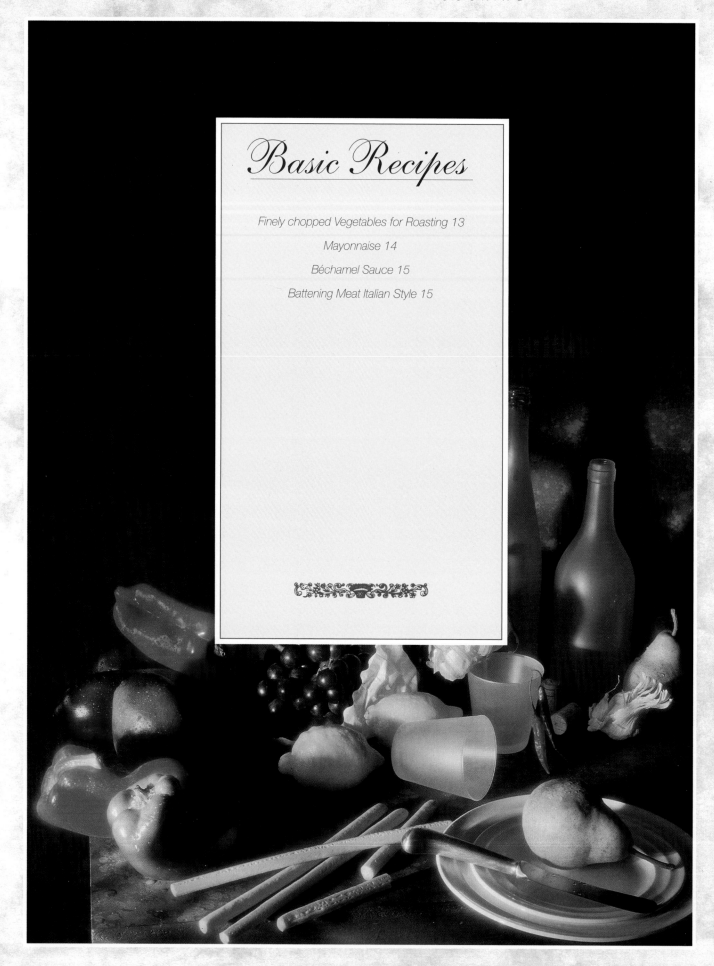

Basic Recipes

Finely Chopped Vegetables for Roasting

TRITTO

This is a pungent, well-seasoned mixture of vegetables preserved in olive oil, which absorbs the tastes of the ingredients and then permeates and lubricates the meat. Kept sealed and reasonably cool, it will keep indefinitely.

How much you make at any time will really depend on the size of your storage jar, which should be of the spring-loaded storage type or have a screw top. My advice is to make as much as possible: you will soon find yourself using it for roasts of all descriptions, and not just Italian ones.

Ample instruction is given in the recipes on the use of *tritto* but the general principle is this: any time you roast or pot-roast meat – and sometimes even fish – spread the *tritto* over and around joint. What the tiny, herb-steeped and caramelized vegetables do to the pan juices is amazing.

The ingredients listed show only proportions, by the way. You could start with 20 onions (followed by 20 carrots) if you wished.

INGREDIENTS
1 medium onion
1 carrot
1 clove garlic
½ stick celery
1 bay leaf
1 spring rosemary
6 fresh sage leaves
Enough olive oil to cover when the ingredients are packed

PREPARATION

▨ *Dice all the ingredients very fine, into ⅛ in dice (or use a food grinder or processor). Sift the pieces together so they are thoroughly mixed.*

▨ *Cover with olive oil. Try not to use for at least 12 hours. (The tritto should be packed quite tightly.)*

Mayonnaise
MAIONESE

| MAKES 1¼ CUPS |
| ½ PT |

Preparation time 10 minutes

INGREDIENTS

2 egg yolks

Juice of half a lemon

1¼ cups / ½ pt olive oil

Salt and freshly ground black pepper
to taste.

PREPARATION

▪ *Vigorously beat the egg yolks with the lemon juice.*
▪ *Begin to introduce the oil in the thinnest stream you can manage. Beat constantly as you do so. (You will see the oil "disappear" into the eggs. It will do so more and more readily as you proceed. Increase the oil flow proportionately.) Season to taste.*

CHEF'S TIPS

The process here is a chemical one known as "emulsification", in which individual molecules of one liquid are held in suspension by another, in this case the oil and egg yolks respectively.
Simply:
▪ Work with ingredients at room temperature, never straight from the refrigerator.
▪ Do not exceed the 2 yolks to 1¼ cups / ½ pt oil relationship. This is all the oil the eggs can "hold."
▪ Go slowly with the oil until you're used to the process. The eggs need a little coaxing to start with.

Béchamel Sauce

BESCIAMELLA

MAKES 2 CUPS / ¾ PT
Preparation time 15 minutes
INGREDIENTS
2 cups/ ¾ pt milk
4 tbsp butter
good ½ cup all-purpose flour
Salt to taste
Pinch of nutmeg (optional but usual in the Italian version)

PREPARATION

■ *Heat the milk until it is almost boiling. While the milk is warming, melt the butter over a low heat and stir in the flour.*
■ *Cook the roux gently for 2 – 3 minutes over a very low heat. The mixture should not color.*
■ *Dribble the milk gently into the roux, stirring as you go. When all the milk is added, bring the liquid to a boil. Keep stirring.*
■ *When the liquid boils, turn down the heat and simmer. Cook for 5 minutes or so. Add salt and nutmeg to taste.*

CHEF'S TIP

Lumps. There is little to fear in this department. If you have proceeded at the prescribed steady pace, there should be none. If there are, either force the sauce through a strainer or liquidize it. Or ignore them altogether: they will cook out later when the sauce is heated for a second time in the dish you intend it for.

Battening Meat Italian Style

This a splendid trick. The toughest meat is rendered tender and the least promising cut can be elevated and extended. It's a great favorite with us *restaurateurs*.
(A word which has no 'n' in it' by the way.)

PREPARATION

■ *Take the piece of meat to be battened. Needless to say, it should be boneless.*
■ *Place it on top of a sheet of plastic wrap on a reasonably sturdy worktop. Place another piece of film on top.*
■ *Working from one side of the meat to the other, set about it with the handiest blunt instrument. A rolling pin will do, although you can buy fancy, flattened battening devices specifically for the purpose. (You must use plastic wrap. Without it, the meat cannot slide and spread easily.)*
The two recipes involving the technique in this book are Veal Escalope with Lemon and Parsley *and* Rolled and Pot Roasted Hare. *But think what else you can do:*
■ *Bone a chicken leg and batten it flat. You will have a very large chicken escalope that can be cooked in seconds, either bread crumbed or sautéed with whatever you fancy.*
■ *Involtini. Escalopes of meat or fish which have been stuffed with a little something, rolled, pinned in position, and then poached or fried. You must be a little delicate when you batten fish, however.*
■ *Portions you might never have considered. The two legs and breasts from one chicken will make 8 very substantial-looking Milanese style escalopes when breadcrumbed.*
This may give you one or two ideas which is really what cooking is all about. But for rather more specific suggestions, read on.

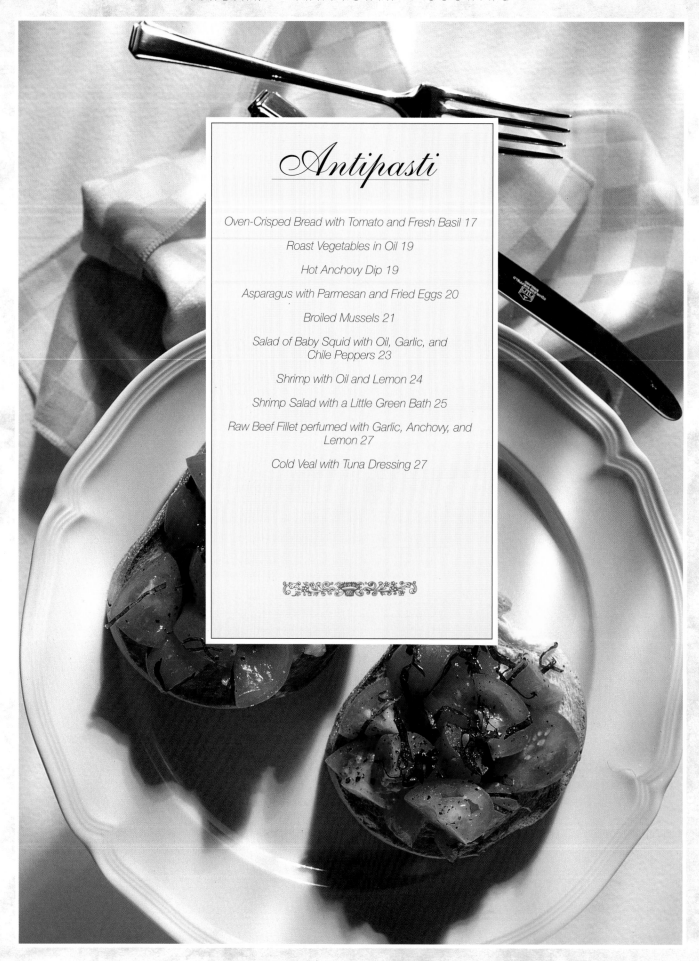

Antipasti

Oven-Crisped Bread with Tomato and Fresh Basil 17

Roast Vegetables in Oil 19

Hot Anchovy Dip 19

Asparagus with Parmesan and Fried Eggs 20

Broiled Mussels 21

*Salad of Baby Squid with Oil, Garlic, and
Chile Peppers 23*

Shrimp with Oil and Lemon 24

Shrimp Salad with a Little Green Bath 25

*Raw Beef Fillet perfumed with Garlic, Anchovy, and
Lemon 27*

Cold Veal with Tuna Dressing 27

Oven-Crisped Bread with Tomato and Fresh Basil

LA BRUSCHETTA

SERVES 6

Preparation time 10 minutes

INGREDIENTS

6 slices thick cut white bread, preferably Italian

1 lb fresh tomatoes

2 oz fresh basil

⅔ cup / ¼ pt olive oil

Salt and freshly ground black pepper to taste

PREPARATION

■ *In a low oven, toast the bread until each slice is completely dry and crisp.*
■ *Roughly dice the tomatoes (there is no need to peel them), and chop the basil fine.*
■ *Add the basil, olive oil, and seasoning to the tomatoes.*
■ *Spoon on top of the bread slices and serve immediately. (The bread should still be slightly warm.)*

CHEF'S TIPS

Think this dish is simple? You are right. As you will learn from this book, Italian cooking attains its elegance through simplicity and not complexity. The ideas work so well because of the basic excellence of the ingredients. That is why the basil *must* be fresh. So either make the dish in season or look for an enterprising supermarket. You may also add a clove of minced garlic at the mixing stage.

Roast Vegetables in Oil
CONTORNI ARROSTI SOTT'OLIO

For an antipasto, allow ½ sweet pepper, ¼ of a medium eggplant, and one zucchini per person.

Cooking time 15 minutes
Oven temperature 375°F
INGREDIENTS
1 yellow, red, or green bell pepper per 2 people
1 eggplant per 4 people
1 zucchini each
⅔ cup / ¼pt olive oil per 4 people
Salt and freshly ground black pepper to taste

PREPARATION

■ *Preheat the oven. Halve the peppers and deseed them. Cut off the coarse stem of the eggplant and trim the zucchini.*
■ *Lay the peppers and eggplant directly on to the oven shelves. Do not baste them. Cook for 10 minutes, then add the zucchini.*
■ *Remove all the vegetables after 15 minutes cooking, when they will be soft.*
■ *Now slice the peppers and eggplants as you will. Simply cut the zucchini in half lengthwise.*

■ *While everything is still hot, brush with the oil and season to taste.*
■ *Pour over what remains of the oil and serve hot, cold, or at room temperature.*

CHEF'S TIP

The vegetables steam in their own juices and thus intensify their own natural goodness. *Basta!*

Hot Anchovy Dip
BAGNA CAUDA

SERVES 6
Preparation time 5 minutes
INGREDIENTS
⅔ cup / ¼pt olive oil
3 tbsp butter
2 cloves garlic, chopped fine
8 anchovy fillets, chopped fine

PREPARATION

■ *Heat the oil and butter together until the butter melts. As soon as the butter begins to foam, add the garlic.*
■ *After 15 seconds or so, add the anchovy fillets and turn the heat down very low.*
■ *Remove the pan from the heat as soon as the fish has disintegrated. Serve warm.*

CHEF'S TIPS

Bagna Cauda is a dip for raw vegetables. Slice whatever you fancy into batons or florets and simply eat 'em up.

Asparagus with Parmesan and Fried Eggs

ASPARAGI ALLA PARMIGIANA CON UOVE FRITTE

SERVES 4
Preparation time 18 – 20 minutes
Oven temperature 375°F
INGREDIENTS
2 lb fresh asparagus
Salt to taste
6 tbsp butter
2 oz freshly grated Parmesan cheese
2 tbsp olive oil
4 eggs

PREPARATION

■ *Preheat the oven. Trim the coarse whitish ends from the asparagus spears.*

■ *Boil the asparagus in salted water for about 10 minutes. (If you can keep the heads above the surface of the water, so much the better. Steamed, they have a better chance of remaining intact.)*

■ *Grease the bottom of a flat, oven-proof dish with one-third of the butter. It should be large enough to accommodate the asparagus in two layers only.*

■ *When the asparagus has cooked, arrange it in the dish.*

■ *Sprinkle the Parmesan over the asparagus and dot it with the remaining butter, then bake until the cheese and butter form a light brown crust – about 10 minutes.*

■ *In the meantime, fry the eggs carefully. You must not break the yolks.*

■ *To serve, divide the asparagus into four portions on heated plates. Slide a fried egg over each portion. The crusty, cheesy asparagus is dipped in the egg yolks and eaten by hand with precious little finesse.*

Broiled Mussels

COZZE ALLA GRIGLIA

SERVES 4 – 6

Preparation time 20 minutes, excluding scrubbing

Oven temperature
(if your broiler is small):
400°F

INGREDIENTS

2 lb fresh mussels

4 oz fresh bread crumbs

2 oz freshly grated Parmesan cheese

4 tbsp parsley, chopped fine

4 large cloves garlic, chopped fine

Salt and pepper to taste

⅔ cup / ¼pt olive oil

PREPARATION

■ Preheat the oven. Thoroughly scrub the mussels, removing all beards and barnacles.

■ Place a pan of water large enough to hold them all on a low heat, add the mussels, and cover. Cook for about 5 minutes.

■ In the meantime, combine the bread crumbs, Parmesan, parsley, garlic, salt, and pepper in a bowl.

■ Take the mussels off the heat, drain, and set aside the liquor.

■ Remove the top shell from each mussel, leaving the flesh in the lower shell. Discard any mussels which have failed to open. Lay the half-shell mussels on a cookie sheet and sprinkle the bread crumb mixture into each shell.

■ Combine the oil and the reserved mussel liquor, and pour a little on to each mussel. Return stuffed mussels to a hot broiler, or the preheated oven, and bake for 3 – 4 minutes.

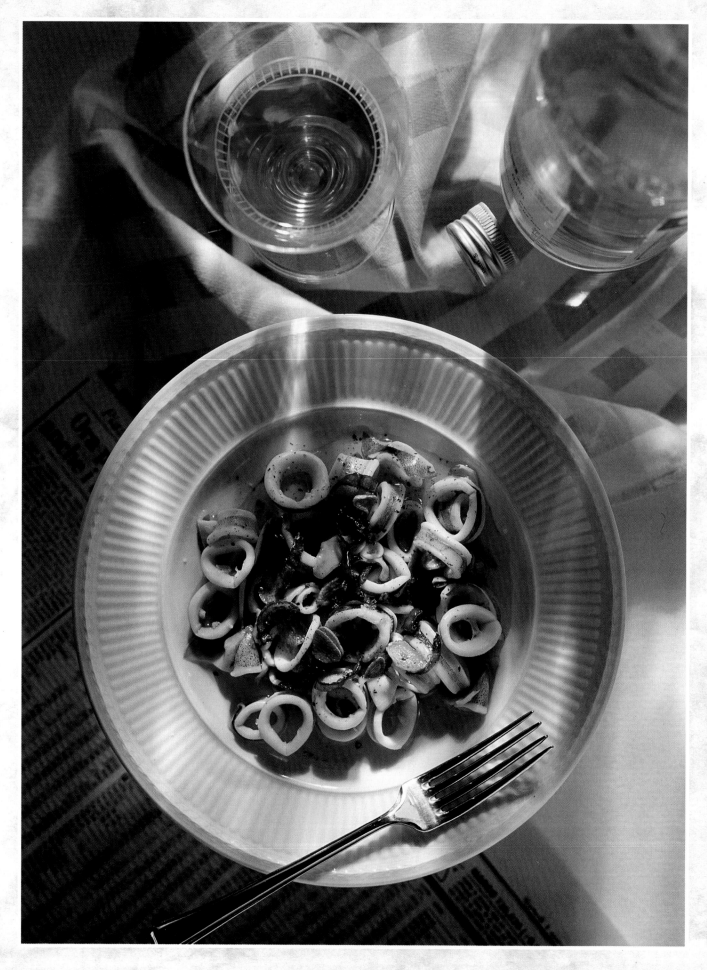

Salad of Baby Squid with Oil, Garlic, and Chile Peppers

INSALATA DI CALAMARETTI AGLIO, OLIO E PEPERONCINI

SERVES 4 – 6

Preparation time 20 minutes

INGREDIENTS

2 lb baby squid

Juice of 1 lemon

1¼ cups / ½ pt olive oil

6 medium cloves garlic, sliced *not* minced

3 green chile peppers, sliced and deseeded

Salt and freshly ground black pepper to taste

PREPARATION

■ *Clean the squid (see Cleaning Squid, p93) and slice the bodies into rings.*

■ *Bring at least 4 times the volume of water as you have squid to a brisk boil. Add the lemon juice.*

■ *Plunge the prepared squid into the boiling water and cook until the flesh loses it translucency. This will take no longer than 1 minute. Immediately remove the squid from the pan and plunge it into cold water to stop the cooking process. (see Chef's Tips)*

■ *In a separate saucepan, heat the olive oil until one piece of garlic sizzles fiercely when dropped in. Add all the garlic. Cook at a high heat for 30 seconds or so, then remove from the heat. The garlic will continue to cook.*

■ *When the garlic pieces have turned mid-brown, add the sliced chile and return the pan to the heat for a further 30 seconds.*

■ *Remove the pan from the heat and allow the cooking to continue. Both garlic and chile should now be dark brown and patently crunchy.*

■ *Allow the oil, garlic, and chile to to cool before you dress the seasoned squid with it.*

CHEF'S TIPS

There are all sorts of subtleties here, and even some cultural stuff into the bargain. But first the subtleties.

Use a large volume of water so that the heat given off, as well as its temperature, remains high. (In physics, heat = mass x temperature. This is why sparks don't burn – although their temperature is high, their mass, and therefore their heat, is relatively low.)

The heat is essential since we wish to cook the squid very quickly, one of the only two ways there are of cooking it. The other way is slowly. Anything in the middle makes it rubbery. Lemon juice is added to whiten the flesh. Do this with any poached fish, if whiteness takes your fancy.

Now for the culture. *Aglio, olio e peperoncini* is an Abruzzese sauce often served with pasta. Abruzzi is a province halfway down the Adriatic coast of Italy, between Ancona and Pescara. The provincial capital is L'Äquila. They use chiles in many dishes. Surprising how hot and spicy Italian food can be, isn't it?

Shrimp with Oil and Lemon

GAMBERETTI ALL 'OLIO E LIMONE

SERVES 4
Preparation time 10 minutes.

INGREDIENTS
1lb smallest fresh shrimp
½ bulb fresh fennel; roughly chopped
1 oz fresh parsley
Juice of 2 lemons
⅔ cup / ¼pt olive oil
Freshly ground black pepper to taste

PREPARATION

■ Bring 4 times as much water by volume as you have shrimp to a rapid boil. See Salad of Baby Squid (p23) and the relevant Chef's Tips.

■ Add the fennel and the parsley and cook for a further 3 – 4 minutes.

■ Drop in the shrimp and cook hard for a further 2 minutes, then drain. Discard the water and the vegetables.

■ Mix the lemon juice and olive oil. Use this to baste the peeled shrimp.

■ Serve, still warm if you can, generously sprinkled with the pepper.

Shrimp Salad with a Little Green Bath

INSALATA DI GAMBERONI AL BAGNETTO VERDE

SERVES 4
Preparation time 15 minutes
INGREDIENTS
2 very large uncooked shrimp
Juice of 1 lemon.
1¼ cup / ½ pt olive oil
2 tbsp fresh parsley
1 oz pine nuts
4 large cloves garlic
6 anchovy fillets
4 capers

PREPARATION

■ Peel the shrimp and remove the dark, thread-line intestine if you can find it. (This is not essential.) Either discard the shells or set them aside to make soup or broth with later. See Zuppa di Pesce.

■ Bring a large quantity of water to a boil – at least 4 times the volume of the shrimp. See Chef's Tips in Salad of Baby Squid (p23).

■ Add the lemon juice and poach the shrimp for 3 – 5 minutes.

■ Remove the shrimp from the liquid and slice them in half lengthwise.

■ There are two ways of making the little green bath. Either put the oil, parsley, pine nuts, garlic, anchovies, and capers into a liquidizer and blend until smooth, or chop parsley, garlic, anchovies, and capers very fine; crush the pine nuts, and briskly stir everything into the oil. (In the case of the latter method, let the mixture stand for 10 minutes or so to enable the flavors to mingle well.)

■ Serve the shrimp with the sauce as a dip.

CHEF'S ASIDE

The *bagnetto verde* is sharper and more piquant than *pesto* (see Noodles with Basil, Pine Nuts, and Parmesan Cheese), which it resembles strongly in method of preparation and appearance. It is stunning. I have a Hungarian friend whose grasp of English is particularly suited to confections like this one. According to him, it would knock you off your socks.

Raw Beef Fillet Perfumed with Garlic, Anchovy, and Lemon

MANZO CRUDO ALLA ZINGARA

SERVES 4

Preparation time 20 minutes

Marinating time 12 hours

INGREDIENTS

1¼ cups / ½ pt olive oil

4 large cloves garlic

4 anchovy fillets

2 whole chile peppers

1 lb fillet steak

Salt and freshly ground black pepper to taste

Juice of 2 lemons

PREPARATION

■ Heat the oil over a low heat until it is hot, but not hot enough to fry.

■ Add the garlic, anchovy fillets, and the chile peppers and let them stew in the oil for 20 minutes. (On no account should there be any sizzle. We are not frying these ingredients but letting their flavors soak out into the oil.)

■ While the marinade is cooking, slice the beef as fine as you can. There is no such thing as too fine. Lay the slices out on a flat dish, lightly salt them, add pepper to taste, and pour over the lemon juice.

■ Remove the oil from the heat after 20 minutes. Allow it to cool then pour it over the beef.

■ Chill the dish for 12 hours. Before serving, remove the garlic and any intact pieces of anchovy. The chiles can be left.

CHEF'S ASIDE

This dish requires a very sharp knife. It is best eaten with unbuttered, very fresh Italian bread, with which you can also mop up the juices.

Cold Veal with Tuna Dressing

VITELLO TONNATO

SERVES 6

Preparation time 20 minutes

INGREDIENTS

1½ lb roast veal (see Roast Veal)

⅔ cup / ¼ pint mayonnaise (see mayonnaise)

3 oz tuna, canned or fresh

⅔ cup / ¼ pt olive oil

3 anchovy fillets

4 capers

2 tablespoons lemon juice

Freshly ground black pepper to taste

PREPARATION

■ Finely slice the roast veal. (It must be cold.)

■ Make the mayonnaise.

■ Either pour the olive oil into a blender and add all the other ingredients except the pepper, veal, and mayonnaise, and blend to a smooth paste, or thoroughly pound the tuna, anchovies, and capers. Add the lemon juice and whisk the mixture into the olive oil.

■ Fold the oil and fish mixture into the mayonnaise.

■ Line the base of a flat dish with a thin coating of the mayonnaise mixture. Top it with a series of veal slices. Dress the veal with more of the mixture and continue until you run out of ingredients.

■ Chill for 2–3 hours before serving. Liberally season this dish with black pepper on its final journey to the table.

CHEF'S ASIDE

Italian cooking is full of historic echoes. The fish and meat combination is one of them. Roman cooking used one particular flavoring very extensively. It was called *garum* and it was, by all accounts, a kind of rotted-down fish paste. Almost every savory dish featured it somewhere, and there were no qualms whatever about intermingling the sea and the land.

Vitello Tonnato, an eerie-sounding combination, demonstrates it perfectly. The dish even appears in France as veal with crayfish sauce. The anchovy, incidentally, is almost certainly *garum's* modern equivalent.

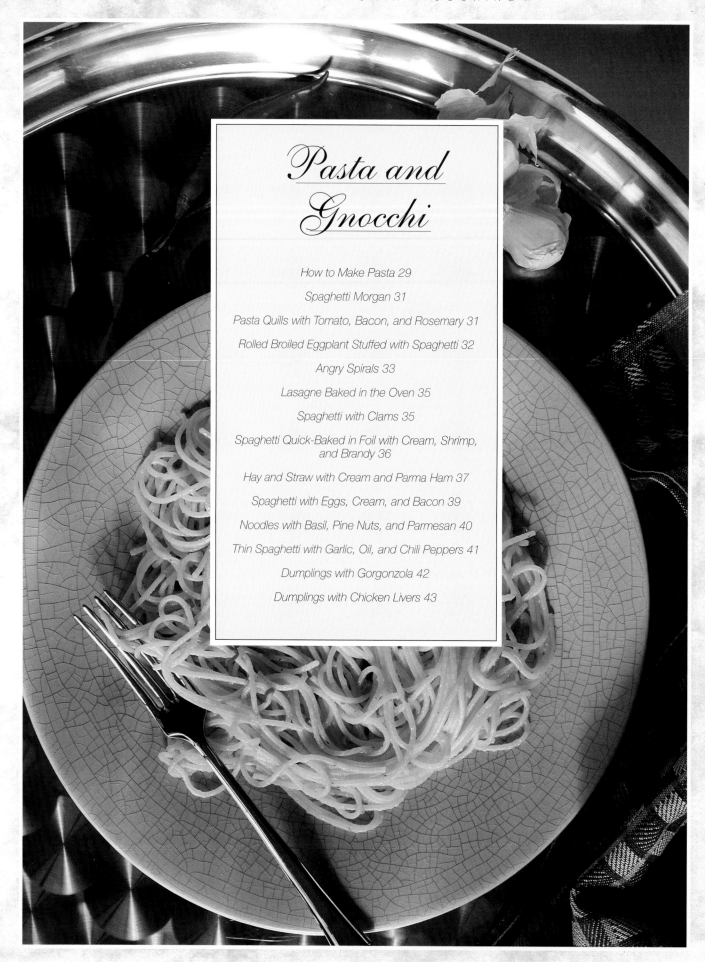

Pasta and Gnocchi

Pasta

Cooking time about 15 minutes

INGREDIENTS

¼ lb dried pasta – *past' asciutta* in Italian

Salt to taste

A little olive oil

PREPARATION

▌ *Use plenty of water when you cook pasta: 3¹/₂ cups/1¹/₂ pt water for every 4oz pasta. Add about ¹/₄ tablespoon of salt per 4 cups/2pts.*

▌ *Drop all the pasta in at once and add a little olive oil to prevent the pasta from sticking.*

▌ *Cover the pot once the pasta has gone in: it will boil sooner. Uncover once a rolling boil has been reached or it will overflow.*

▌ *Cook the pasta al dente. The instant it is cooked, drain it, add the desired sauce and serve it, unless it is going on into the oven. (see* Spaghetti al Cartoccio *and* Lasagne al Forno, *p35).*

▌ *Now see Chef's Tips for home-made pasta.*

CHEF'S TIPS

Pasta is made simply from bread flour, water and salt, with the occasional addition of oil and eggs. The dough is child's play and, although the shapes can be rolled out by hand, I would recommend buying one of the small, stainless steel hand-cranked pasta machines now commonly available. Since they do not get hot like electric machines, they have no tendency to dry the dough as they roll it. And in any event, making pasta by hand, though time-consuming, is highly therapeutic. Kids love to get involved, too.

INGREDIENTS (PER PERSON)

3oz bread flour

A pinch of salt

1 tsp olive oil

1 beaten egg (optional)

About 4 tbsp water

PREPARATION

▌ Sift the flour and salt together. Make a well in the middle of the flour and pour in the oil – and the egg if you wish. If you are not using egg, pour in the water.

▌ Fold the flour and the wet ingredients together and knead thoroughly until they are well mixed.

▌ Let the dough stand for a few minutes, wrapped to keep the moisture in. Roll out or feed into your machine.

▌ Remember that the cooking time for fresh pasta is more accurately measured in seconds than minutes.

Spaghetti Morgan
SPAGHETTI AL MORGAN

SERVES 6

Cooking time 45 minutes

INGREDIENTS

1 lb dried spaghetti

Salt to taste

1¼ cups / ½ pt olive oil

3 cloves garlic

1 medium onion

2 lb fresh plum or canned tomatoes

1tsp sugar

1 large eggplant

2 tbsp fresh basil, chopped fine,(one-third quantity, if using dried)

PREPARATION

■ *Set to boil 7pt water and salt it. As the water is heating, heat 4 tbsp olive oil in a deep skillet. Crush the garlic, slice the onions, and soften them together in the oil.*

■ *Roughly chop the tomatoes and add them to the onion mixture when it is softened. Add the sugar and turn the heat down to simmer.*

■ *In a deepish pan, heat the remaining olive oil until just below smoking temperature. As the oil heats up, cut the eggplant into small ¼ in dice.*

■ *Fry the eggplant dice, a batch at a time, until the flesh is cooked to a wrinkled mid-brown. Set aside the cooked pieces on paper towels.*

■ *Cook the pasta until al dente; drain.*

■ *Stir the eggplant into the tomato sauce and throw in the finely chopped basil. Check the seasoning and serve with the pasta immediately.*

CHEF'S ASIDE

The pungent flavor of the crisped eggplant and the fresh and practically uncooked strands of basil make this sauce truly special. It comes originally from Sicily, where it was probably named after the pirate.

Pasta Quills with Tomato, Bacon, and Rosemary
PENNE ALL'AMATRICIANA CON ROSMARINO

SERVES 6

Cooking time 40 minutes

INGREDIENTS

1 lb penne

Salt to taste

2 tbsp olive oil

3 cloves garlic

1 medium onion

¼ lb bacon or *pancetta*, roughly chopped

2 lb fresh or canned plum tomatoes

1 tsp suger

2 tsp fresh rosemary, chopped fine

PREPARATION

■ *Prepare the pasta in the normal manner.*

■ *Cook the onions, and garlic in the oil as for* Spaghetti al Morgan.

■ *Add the bacon and heat it gently for 2–3 minutes. Stir in the tomatoes and sugar. Simmer the sauce for 15–20 minutes. Add the rosemary to the sauce 5 minutes before serving.*

■ *Season and serve.*

Rolled Broiled Eggplant Stuffed with Spaghetti

INVOLTINI DI MELANZANE E SPAGHETTI

SERVES 6
Cooking time about 30 minutes
Oven temperature 375°F
INGREDIENTS
2 medium eggplants
1 lb spaghetti
Salt
4 tbsp olive oil
3 cloves garlic
1 medium onion
2 lb fresh or canned plum tomatoes
1 tsp sugar
2 tbsp basil, chopped fine (one-third the quantity if using dried)
3 tbsp freshly grated Parmesan cheese

PREPARATION

■ *Preheat the oven. Slice the eggplants lengthwise into ¹/₂ in strips. Roast them as for* Contorni Arrosti, p19.

■ *Prepare the pasta in the normal manner.*
■ *Cook half the oil together with the garlic, onion, sugar, and tomatoes as for* Spaghetti al Morgan, p31. *Add the basil, however, as soon as the sauce is cooked in about 20 minutes.*
■ *When the pasta is cooked, drain it and allow it to cool a little – but only a little. (If it were any hotter, it would burn you.)*
■ *Top each slice of eggplant with a thin layer of pasta. Spread tomato sauce on top of that. Roll the eggplant slice up into a long bundle. Secure it with a toothpick.*

■ *Arrange the bundles on a cookie sheet and brush them with the remaining oil. Sprinkle with the Parmesan, return to the oven, and bake until the cheese forms a light crust on top of the involtini.*
■ *When serving, spoon over what remains of the sauce.*

Angry Spirals
FUSILLI ARRABIATI

SERVES 4 – 6

Preparation time about 25 minutes

INGREDIENTS

1 lb spiral pasta – fusilli

Salt

2 tbsp olive oil

2 cloves garlic

1 medium onion

2 lb fresh or canned plum tomatoes

1 tsp sugar

2 tsp finely chopped fresh basil (one-third the quantity, if using dried)

2 fresh chile peppers

PREPARATION

■ *Prepare the pasta in the usual manner.*
■ *Prepare a tomato sauce, using the garlic, onion, tomatoes, sugar, and basil as for* Spaghetti al Morgan, *p31.*
■ *As the sauce is cooking, slice and deseed the chiles. Add them to the sauce 5 minutes before you are ready to serve it.*
■ *Drain the pasta, toss it with the sauce, and carry on.*

CHEF'S TIP

Chiles leave a good deal of their potency on the fingers that peel them. So be careful what you touch afterwards – eyes, for example – or wear gloves.

Lasagne Baked in the Oven
LASAGNE AL FORNO

SERVES 6

Preparation time (with
past'asciutta) 40 minutes

Oven temperature
425°F

INGREDIENTS

1 lb dried lasagne

Salt

4 tbsp olive oil

2 cloves garlic

1 medium onion

2 lb fresh or canned plum
tomatoes

1 tsp sugar

2 tbsp fresh basil
(one-third the quantity,
if using dried)

1 pt béchamel (see
Béchamel Sauce, p15)

PREPARATION

■ *Preheat the oven. Cook the strips of lasagne until just soft in a large pan of boiling water and a little olive oil. Remove from the water, drain them, and lay them out, not overlapping, on a lightly greased work surface.*
■ *Using a little over half the oil, make a tomato sauce as for Spaghetti al Morgan, p31.*
■ *Grease the bottom of a 12-in, baking dish with the remaining oil. Cover it with a layer of the cooked pasta.*
■ *Spoon a layer of the tomato sauce on to the pasta, followed by a layer of the béchamel. Proceed thus until the dish is full: pasta, sauce, béchamel, pasta, sauce, and so on. (Ensure you retain sufficient béchamel for a generous final coating.)*
■ *Bake in the very hot oven for 15 – 20 minutes, or until the top has browned well and begun to crisp at the edges.*

CHEF'S TIPS

Baking pasta is a
commonplace and you
can do it with all kinds
and with many sauces.
Simply make sure the
pasta is well sauced and
covered or it will dry out.

Spaghetti with Clams
SPAGHETTI ALLE VONGOLE

SERVES 4

Cooking time about
25 minutes

INGREDIENTS

1 lb spaghetti

Salt to taste

1 lb fresh clams

2 tbsp olive oil

1 clove garlic, minced

1 medium onion, sliced fine

2 anchovy fillets, chopped

14 oz plum or canned
tomatoes roughly chopped

1 tbsp fresh parsley,
chopped fine

Freshly grated black pepper

PREPARATION

■ *Cook the pasta in the usual way. The sauce will take about 25 minutes, so begin it about 5 – 10 minutes later.*
■ *Put the clams in a pan with a close-fitting lid. Cook them very gently over a medium heat for 3 – 4 minutes. Remove from the heat and discard any that have failed to open. Detach the rest from their shells, rinse them to remove any sand, and set aside. Strain the clam juices left in the pan and add them to the bowl with the clams.*
■ *Heat the olive oil and add the garlic and the onion. Soften them together for 3 – 4 minutes without allowing them to color. Then add the anchovy fillets and the tomatoes. Cook the sauce for 15 minutes or so.*
■ *When the pasta is cooked, drain it and set it on a warm serving dish. Turn the heat under the sauce to high and, as it begins to spit, throw in the clams and the parsley. Check the salt, twist in a generous swirl of the pepper, pour over the pasta, and begin.*

CHEF'S TIP

It is traditional not to
serve Parmesan with
seafood dishes. This one
is no exception.

Spaghetti Quick-Baked in Foil with Cream, Shrimp, and Brandy

SPAGHETTI AL CARTOCCIO CON GAMBERONI

SERVES 6

Cooking time 30 minutes

Oven temperature
375°F

INGREDIENTS

1 lb spaghetti

Salt to taste

1¼ cups / ½ pt heavy cream

2 tbsp fresh parsley,
chopped fine

4 tbsp brandy or cognac

½ lb peeled uncooked
shrimp (cooked can be
substituted, if necessary)

Freshly grated black pepper

PREPARATION

■ *Preheat the oven. Set the pasta to cook in the usual manner on top of the stove.*

■ *As the pasta is cooking, bring the cream to a boil in a saucepan. Add the parsley to the cream, together with the cognac.*

■ *Remove the cream from the heat. Let it stand so that the flavors infuse.*

■ *Now chop the shrimp fine. If they are uncooked, add them to the cream and return it to the heat until it boils again. There is no need to bring cooked shrimp to a boil.*

■ *When you are ready to drain the pasta, spread out on a cookie sheet a sheet of foil large enough to fold over and completely envelop both pasta and sauce. Place the drained pasta in the middle of the foil and pour the sauce on top. Lift the edges of the foil upwards around the pasta and fold them together completely sealing the contents.*

■ *Bake the parcel in the hot oven for about 5 minutes then transfer the foil intact to a serving dish.*

■ *Unseal at the table, sprinkle with black pepper, and serve.*

Hay and Straw with Cream and Parma Ham

PAGLIA E FIENO CON PROSCIUTTO PANNA

SERVES 4
Cooking time about 20 minutes

INGREDIENTS

½ lb plain noodles

½ lb spinach noodles

Salt

1¼ cups / ½ pt heavy cream

1 tbsp fresh sage, chopped fine

1 tbsp fresh parsley, chopped fine

⅔ cup / ¼ pint dry white wine

¼ lb Parma ham

2 tbsp butter

PREPARATION

■ *Cook the pastas in the usual way.*
■ *Bring the cream to a boil, add the sage, parsley, and white wine. Keep boiling to reduce the volume of liquid by one-third to the original volume of the cream.*
■ *When this is done, dice the ham and add it to the cream. Remove from the heat.*
■ *When the pasta is cooked, drain it, and whisk in the butter. Toss it in the mixture and serve very hot*

Spaghetti with Eggs, Cream, and Bacon

SPAGHETTI ALLA CARBONARA

SERVES 4 – 6
Cooking time 20 minutes

INGREDIENTS
1 lb spaghetti
Salt
6 eggs, thoroughly beaten
2 tbsp olive oil
¼ lb Parma ham
1 tbsp parsley, chopped fine
4 tbsp heavy cream
As much freshly grated black pepper as you can take

PREPARATION

■ Prepare the pasta in the usual manner.

■ Heat the olive oil and crisp the Parma ham in it. Add the parsley, and cook for a minute or so over a high heat. Remove from the heat.

■ When the pasta is cooked, drain it. Immediately add the eggs and the ham, parsley, and pan juices. Stir the spaghetti briskly so that its latent heat cooks the eggs on to the strands.

■ Add the cream only when the eggs have properly scrambled; the dish must on no account be too liquid.

■ Serve with a very generous helping of the pepper. Very hot, of course.

Noodles with Basil, Pine Nuts, and Parmesan Cheese

TAGLIATELLE AL PESTO

SERVES 6

Cooking time about
20 minutes

INGREDIENTS

1 lb noodles

Salt

¼ lb fresh basil leaves
(dried just will not do)

⅔ cup / ¼ pt olive oil

3 tbsp pine nuts

2 cloves garlic

⅓ cup freshly grated
Parmesan cheese

3 tbsp freshly grated
Pecorino cheese (optional)

PREPARATION

■ *Prepare the pasta in the usual way.*
■ *Put all the ingredients except the cheeses in the blender; process to a fine paste. If you have no blender, you must use a mortar and pestle. In this case, add the olive oil after you have blended all the other ingredients.*
■ *Whisk in the cheeses by hand and only then check the salt: the cheeses may well be salty enough. (You may blend the cheeses along with the other ingredients, if you wish, but you will find the texture rather too smooth if you do.)*
■ *When the pasta is ready, drain it and toss it in the pesto. Mangiatelo subito!*

Thin Spaghetti with Garlic, Oil, and Chile Peppers

CAPELLI D'ANGELI AGLIO, OLIO E PEPERONCINI

SERVES 4

Cooking time about 20 minutes

INGREDIENTS

1 lb fine spaghetti

Salt to taste

1¼ cups / ½ pt olive oil

8 cloves of garlic

4 chile peppers

PREPARATION

■ *Plunge the pasta into about 7 pts of boiling water. Add salt to taste and add a splash of olive oil.*
■ *With the remaining ingredients, make the aglio, olio, and peperoncini dressing. (See* Insalata di Calamaretti, *p23.)*
■ *When the pasta is cooked al dente, drain it and toss it in the dressing. Serve immediately.*

CHEF'S ASIDE

This is *my* favorite pasta dish. Exquisite is a poor attempt to describe this Abruzzese specialty.

Dumplings with Gorgonzola

GNOCCHI AL GORGONZOLA

SERVES 4 – 6

Cooking time about
15 minutes

INGREDIENTS

1 lb potato gnocchi (see
Chef's Tip)

Salt

1 cup / ⅓ pt milk

4 tbsp butter

¼ lb Gorgonzola,
crumbled into tiny pieces

2 tbsp freshly grated
Parmesan cheese

4 tbsp heavy cream

PREPARATION

■ *Boil the gnocchi as you would pasta. But watch as they will cook more quickly – 3 to 4 minutes should be quite sufficient.*

■ *As the gnocchi are cooking, heat the milk in a pan large enough to hold all the ingredients, including the gnocchi. As soon as the milk is warm, reduce the heat to a low simmer. Add the butter, the crumbled Gòrgonzola, and the Parmesan. Slowly beat everything into a creamy paste. Remove from the heat.*

■ *As soon as the pasta is cooked, drain it and add it to the sauce. Over a very low heat, stir in the cream. Serve this luxury number instantly.*

CHEF'S TIP

INGREDIENTS FOR POTATO GNOCCHI

1½ lb boiling
potatoes

1 cup bread flour

Salt to taste

■ Boil the potatoes in their skins until they are just soft. Peel them as soon as you can, and blend – or mash – them while still warm.

■ Work in the flour, sifted with a little salt, until you have a pliable, sticky dough.

■ Chop the dough into thumb-size pieces. Press each one gently with a floured fork to flatten and serrate it.

Dumplings with Chicken Livers

GNOCCHI CON FEGATI DI POLLO

SERVES 4 – 6
Cooking time 20 minutes

INGREDIENTS
1 lb potato gnocchi
Salt
2 tbsp olive oil
2 cloves of garlic
1 small onion, chopped very fine
1 tbsp fresh sage, chopped fine
⅔ cup / ¼ pt red wine
½ lb chicken livers
⅔ cup / ¼ pt heavy cream

PREPARATION

■ Cook the gnocchi in the usual manner.
■ Heat the oil in a skillet, throw in the whole cloves of garlic and the onion. Soften in the oil until the onion begins to brown.
■ Add the sage and the red wine; reduce the volume of the wine by half over a high heat. Remove.
■ When all the gnocchi are ready, bring the red wine mixture back to a boil and toss in the livers, chopped very fine. Cook for a minute or so, then add the cream.
■ Bring the pan back to a boil, check the seasoning, and off the heat, gently stir in the gnocchi. Serve right away.

Risotto, Polenta, and Pizza

Black Risotto with Cuttlefish

RISOTTO NERO ALLE SEPPIE

SERVES 4
Cooking time 25 – 30 minutes
Preparation 10 minutes
INGREDIENTS
1 large cuttlefish (about 2 lb)
3 tbsp olive oil
1 large onion, sliced fine
2 cloves garlic, minced
4 tbsp tomato paste
2/3 cup / 1/4 pt red wine
3/4 lb risotto rice
Salt and pepper to taste
1 lemon

PREPARATION

■ *First, clean the cuttlefish (see Chef's Tips). Make very sure you reserve the ink sac. Now slice both body and tentacles very finely indeed and set them aside. (If your fish is truly inky, the chopping board will be an interesting new colour: black.)*

■ *To soak up the excess ink, peel and finely slice the onion on the same board.*

■ *Heat half the oil in a pan over a medium heat and add half the onion and the garlic, and cook both until soft. Now add the cuttlefish slices. Stir in the tomato paste and the red wine.*

■ *As the mixture cooks, either empty the ink-sac contents into it or, if the contents of the sac are hard, chop the sac and ink as well as you can. (This can be difficult, for they are often a little sticky and clinging.) Add to the pan when chopped.*

■ *Add the water in which you have cleaned the fish (see Chef's Tip). Braise the fish mixture until the volume has reduced by about half: 25 minutes or so.*

■ *As the fish is cooking, bring 3 1/2 cups/1 1/2 pt water to a boil in another saucepan.*

■ *While the water is boiling, soften the remainder of the onion in the rest of the oil in another pan and add the rice. Toast it lightly.*

■ *Pour the water on to the rice and onion mixture, and boil for about 15 minutes until the rice is ready. Drain immediately and fold it into the fish.*

■ *Serve the cuttlefish risotto very hot, seasoned if necessary. Garnish with a bright yellow wedge of lemon – very striking against the black.*

CHEF'S TIPS

Clean the cuttlefish in as small a bowl of cold water as it and your hands will fit: it will leak ink and you will want to catch this precious substance.

To clean, hold the body in one hand and tentacles in the other. Pull gently and the two will part company. Now cut the tentacles away just above where they join the head and lay them on the chopping board. We shall return to them later. At the moment we are looking for ink.

The sac is tear-drop shaped and about the size of an average thumb. It lies at the back of the head and will be covered by a greyish-pink membrane, but its black contents will clearly show through. If ink is obscuring your view, wash the head carefully in clean water. Be careful with the sac: sometimes the contents are liquid, so cut it away over the bowl of water and let the contents fall in. Now discard the rest of the head.

The outer body is a simple business. Remove the cuttle bone – you can't miss it – and lay the flesh next to the tentacles. Pick up your best knife and start slicing.

Sounds gruesome? This is an extraordinary dish. Cuttlefish ink makes the ink of the squid look like milk. But the flavor it gives to the rice is immensely subtle and perfumed. This is the best risotto I know. And certainly the most dramatic. *Buon' Appetito!*

Risotto with Dried Ceps

RISOTTO COI FUNGHI PORCINI SECCHI

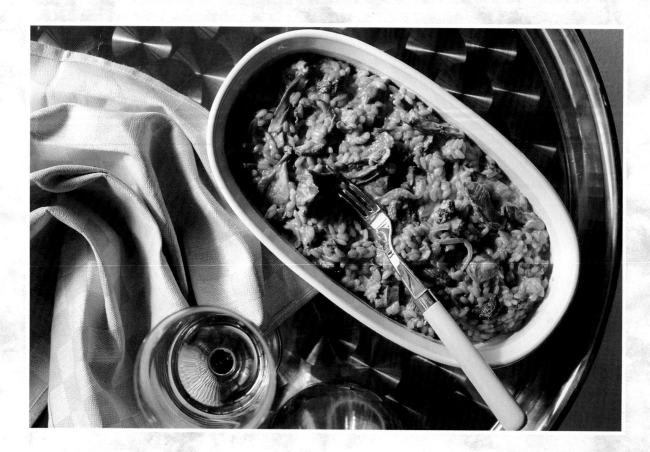

SERVES 4 – 6

Preparation time about 20 minutes

Marinating time at least half an hour

INGREDIENTS

2 oz dried ceps (*see* Chef's Tips)

1¼ cups / ½ pt dry white wine

1 chicken bouillon cube (*see* Pastine in Brodo, p59)

1 small onion

4 tbsp olive oil

14 oz risotto rice

⅔ cup / ¼ pt heavy cream

3 tbsp freshly grated Parmesan cheese

Salt and freshly grated black pepper to taste

PREPARATION

■ *Put the ceps in a pan and cover them with the white wine. Crumble the bouillon cube over them and add 4 ¼ cups/1¾ pt water.*

■ *Poach the ceps gently in the broth and wine until they are soft and swollen. Strain them carefully and reserve the poaching liquid. Wash the ceps once or twice more in fresh water: they can be gritty.*

■ *To remove grit from the poaching liquid, strain it too, through either cheesecloth or a very fine strainer.*

■ *Boil the poaching liquid briskly. Your aim is to reduce its volume by about one-third and consequently intensify its flavor.*

■ *As the mushroom broth boils, slice the onion fine then soften it in a sturdy pan with the oil. Add the rice and toast it with the oil and onion.*

■ *Pour the mushroom liquid over the rice and let it cook until the liquid is almost absorbed. If this happens before the rice is cooked – about 15 minutes – add small amounts of water. Not too much.*

■ *When the rice is cooked – al dente, naturally – stir in the cream and cheese; check the seasoning. Just before serving stir in the mushrooms.*

CHEF'S TIPS

Dried ceps are available in all good Italian food stores. As you will have gathered, the Italian for ceps is *funghi porcini*. They are highly prized, as well they should be.

Artichoke Risotto

RISOTTO AI CARCIOFINI

SERVES 4

Preparation time about 20 minutes

INGREDIENTS

4 tbsp butter

1 small onion, sliced fine

¾ lb risotto rice

2 chicken bouillon cubes (*see* Pastine in Brodo, 59)

2 cans artichoke hearts (*see* Chef's Tips)

4 tbsp heavy cream

3 tbsp freshly grated Parmesan cheese

Salt and pepper to taste

PREPARATION

◼ *Melt the butter in a sturdy pan. Soften the onion in it. Add the rice and toast it for 2 – 3 minutes. (Do not allow anything to color.)*
◼ *Crumble in the bouillon cube and add 4 cups / 2 pt water.*
◼ *Cook the rice until it is al dente. If too much liquid remains in the pan, ladle it out.*
◼ *As the rice is cooking, drain and wash the artichokes. Gently warm them with the cream and the grated Parmesan. Fold this mixtute into the rice as soon as it is cooked. Season and serve imediately.*

CHEF'S TIPS

The dish originates with the baby artichokes – which can be eaten whole, choke and all – in season in Italy during very early spring. If you can find them, use them. Regrettably, they are very rare outside the country. However, they do point up a principle enshrined in the conclusion of this book, to which you are duly referred.

Risotto with Two Cheeses

RISOTTO AI DUE FORMAGGI

SERVES 4
Preparation time about 25 minutes

INGREDIENTS
4 tbsp butter
1 medium onion, sliced fine
11 oz risotto rice
2 chicken bouillon cubes (*see* Pastine in Brodo, p59)
½ cup fresh grated Parmesan cheese
⅔ cup / ¼ pt heavy cream
½ cup crumbled Gorgonzola
Salt and freshly grated black pepper to taste

PREPARATION

■ *Melt the butter in a sturdy pan and soften the onion in it. Add the rice and toast it for 2 – 3 minutes.*

■ *Crumble in the bouillon cubes and add 4 cups/1½ pt water. Cook the rice until it is al dente. Add the Parmesan.*

■ *As the rice is cooking, warm the cream and add the crumbled Gorgonzola to it. Stir until the cheese has thoroughly melted.*

■ *When the rice is cooked, whisk in the cream and Gorgonzola, season, and serve very hot.*

How To Make Polenta
COME FARE POLENTA

SERVES 4 – 6

Cooking time about 30 minutes

INGREDIENTS

¾ lb coarse-grained cornmeal

Salt

PREPARATION

▮ Bring 7½ cups/3 pt water to a boil in a heavy saucepan. (Polenta will tend to stick to thin pans.) Turn the water down to a simmer.

▮ Pour the meal to run into water in a very thin stream. (Try counting the grains!) Stir continuously.

▮ Once all the grain has been added, keep stirring. This is a job that will take you 20 minutes.

▮ Like couscous, the polenta is cooked when it can be lifted away from the sides of the pan as you stir. It should easily hold the shape of the spoon. Just before it reaches this point add salt.

▮ Either serve the polenta immediately, very hot, or pour it out on to a shallow dish. When cooled and set (which takes about 2 – 3 hours), it can be sliced and further transformed.

Polenta with Butter and Cheese
POLENTA CON BURRO E PARMIGIANO

SERVES 6

Cooking time about 30 minutes

INGREDIENTS

¾ lb hot, cooked polenta (see How To Make Polenta)

6 oz butter

⅓ cup freshly grated Parmesan cheese

A little boiling water (about ⅔ cup / ¼ pt)

Generous amount black pepper

PREPARATION

▮ When the polenta is just cooked, pour it on to a hot serving dish.

▮ Mix in the butter and the cheese immediately, adding a little hot water if the mixture is very thick.

▮ Season generously with black pepper. Serve very hot.

Broiled Polenta with Gorgonzola

POLENTA ALLA GRIGLIA CON GORGONZOLA

SERVES 6

Preparation time 5 minutes

INGREDIENTS

¾ lb cooked and cooled polenta (*see* How To Make Polenta)

½ lb Gorgonzola cheese

PREPARATION

■ Cut the cold, set polenta into manageable blocks and carefully cut each block into 1-in slices.

■ Heat the broiler to maximum and toast each slice on both sides, until the surface begins to brown and bubble.

■ Spread one side of each polenta slice with the Gorgonzola. Return it to the broiler.

■ Serve as soon as the cheese has melted

Fried Polenta with Mushrooms

POLENTA FRITTA CON FUNGHI

SERVES 6

Cooking time about 20 minutes

INGREDIENTS

2 tbsp olive oil

2 tbsp butter

1½ lb field or wood mushrooms or ceps (*funghi porcini*), roughly chopped

2 cloves of garlic, roughly chopped

2 whole small chile peppers, roughly chopped

1 medium tomato, roughly diced

4 tbsp red wine

1 tbsp fresh parsley, chopped fine

1 tbsp fresh sage, chopped fine

Salt and pepper to taste

PREPARATION

■ Melt one-third of the oil and the butter together over a medium heat.

■ Add the mushrooms, garlic, and chiles and fry together for 3 – 4 minutes over a high heat.

■ Add the wine, tomatoes, parsley, and sage to the mixture. Reduce the heat to a simmer.

■ As the mixture is cooking, slice the cold polenta as for broiled polenta. (see Broiled Polenta)

■ In a large, open pan, heat the remaining oil over a high heat.

■ Fry each slice on both sides until a thin crust forms. Keep the slices hot if you do the frying in more than one batch.

■ When all the polenta is fried, season the mushroom mixture and spoon it generously over each slice.

■ Eat it hot.

Pizza Dough
PASTA PER LA PIZZA

SERVES 6 – 8
Preparation time 10 minutes
Rising time 3 – 4 hours
INGREDIENTS
1 oz. dried yeast (twice the quantity if using fresh)
2 lb bread flour
4 tbsp olive oil
Salt to taste

PREPARATION

■ Heat $^2/_3$ cup/$^1/_4$ pt water until it is just hot enough to bathe a baby. Add the yeast and stir well. Let the mixture stand until it begins to foam.

■ Pile the flour in a heap on a suitable work surface. Season it and make a well in the middle.

■ Have ready $2^1/_2$ cups/1 pt barely lukewarm water; place it alongside the flour.

■ Pour the yeast mixture into the well and add the olive oil. Work quickly: mix yeast, water and dough – don't use your stand-by water yet – until the consistency is even. The dough will be too dry, of course. It is now that you begin to work in the extra water. The dough should be firm and supple. Stop when you reach this point.

■ Now put the dough in a floured, or lightly oiled, bowl. Cover and leave in a warm place for at least three hours. When the dough has doubled in volume, it is ready to use. (There is no need to re-knead.)

Mozzarella and Tomato Pizza
PIZZA MARGUERITA

SERVES 6 – 8
Preparation time 20 minutes
Oven temperature 350°F
INGREDIENTS
Pizza dough made with 2 lb flour (see Pizza Dough)
1 lb fresh or canned plum tomatoes
1 lb fresh Mozzarella cheese
2 tbsp fresh oregano, chopped fine (half the quantity if using dried)
$^2/_3$ cup / $^1/_4$ pt olive oil
Salt and freshly ground black pepper

PREPARATION

■ Preheat the oven. Divide the dough into six even portions. Roll each out to a thickness of $^1/_4$ in.

■ Finely chop the tomatoes and spread them evenly over the pastry bases.

■ Grate the Mozzarella and spread it over the tomatoes. Sprinkle the oregano over it. Then sprinkle the olive oil over that.

■ Season and bake in the preheated oven for about 15 minutes, until the dough has risen slightly and the cheese has melted and browned.

Pizza As You Like It

PIZZA CAPRICCIOSA

SERVES 6 – 8
Preparation time 30 minutes
Oven temperature 350°F

INGREDIENTS
Pizza dough made with 2 lb flour (*see* Pizza Dough, p55)
1 lb fresh or tinned plum tomatoes
1 lb Mozzarella
12 anchovy fillets
2 tbsp capers
½ lb salami, sliced fine
½ lb mushrooms, sliced fine
24 artichoke hearts
2 tbsp fresh oregano, chopped fine
⅔ cup / ¼ pt olive oil
Salt and freshly ground black pepper

PREPARATION

■ Preheat the oven. Proceed as though making Pizza Marguerita up to – but not including – the oregano-sprinkling stage.

■ Arrange even quantities of the anchovies, capers, salami, mushrooms, and artichoke hearts on top of each pizza.

■ Now sprinkle with the oregano and olive oil. Season and bake for about 15 minutes.

CHEF'S TIP

Capricciosa, "according to our whim," can be anything. Try seafood, or a variety of cheeses, or simply mushrooms, or sweet peppers. You can leave out the capers, too. I always do!

Corn Bread with Olives

FOCACCIA

SERVES ABOUT 6
Preparation time 1 hour
Oven temperature 400°F

INGREDIENTS
¾ lb bread flour
¼ lb very fine semolina flour
5 tbsp fresh yeast
⅔ cup / ¼ pt olive oil
Salt to taste
⅔ cup / ¼ pt milk
2 oz green olives

PREPARATION

■ Sift the two flours together. Mix the yeast with a very little warm water. When it begins to foam, work it into the flours with a quarter of the olive oil and the salt. Blend all the ingredients very thoroughly.

■ Heat the milk. It is hot enough when bubbles begin to show around the edges of the pan.

■ Combine the milk and the flour and yeast mixture – if you have a mixer with a dough hook, so much the better. Fold in the olives.

■ Cover the dough and let it stand in a warm place for about 30 minutes. Then remove and shape into a flat, round loaf.

■ Lightly oil a cookie sheet with some of the remaining oil and place the loaf on it. Brush the rest generously over the dough.

■ Bake in the preheated oven for about 25 minutes until the top is a handsome shade of brown.

CHEF'S TIP

Eat this delectable item as hot as you can handle it. It goes superbly with a big plate of Italian hams and salamis – known as *affettato misto* to the *cognoscenti*.

Soup

Tiny Pasta in Broth 59

Rice and Peas 60

Poached Egg in Broth 61

Vegetable Soup 63

Garbanzo Bean Soup 64

Bean Soup with Parsley, Garlic, and Chile 65

Lentil Soup 66

Potato and Onion Soup 67

Red Lettuce and Rice Soup with Fresh Sage 68

Mussel Soup 69

Tiny Pasta in Broth
PASTINE IN BRODO

SERVES 4 – 6
Cooking time about 3 hours

INGREDIENTS

1 medium onion
1 large carrot
2 stalks celery
1 small fennel bulb
½ medium green bell pepper
1 medium potato
1 ripe fresh tomato (about ¼ lb)
2 lb assorted meat scraps and bones
½ lb dried pasta stars
Salt and pepper to taste

PREPARATION

■ Put all the ingredients except the pasta and the salt into 7 cups/2 ¾ pt cold water.

■ Bring the liquid very slowly to just under a boil and hold it there. (Boiling makes broth cloudy, so don't.) Cook for 3 hours. Skim the broth constantly, or, when it is cooked, allow to cool and then lift off the solidfied fats. (This will considerably lengthen the preparation process.)

■ When the broth is cooked and skimmed, add the pasta. Since you have carefully removed all the fats, you may now boil it. Do so for about 10 minutes, or until the pasta shells are just soft. Season and serve.

CHEF'S TIP

It is only the truly assiduous who teach themselves broth making. For that reason, you will find frequent references to bouillon cubes as you proceed. Of course, a better substitute in all cases is the home-made article and the above is how the Italians do it. You will note that it is very light and delicate. Please keep it that way – in the refrigerator if you wish. Use it as often as you can in place of cubes.

Rice and Peas

RISI E BISI

SERVES 4
Cooking time 20 minutes
INGREDIENTS
4 tbsp butter
1 tbsp olive oil
1 small onion
2 lb fresh peas, shelled (*see* Cook's Tips)
1 bouillon cube (*see* Pastine in Brodo *Chef's Tip*, p59)
½ lb risotto rice
2 tbsp fresh parsley, chopped fine
⅓ cup freshly grated Parmesan
Salt and pepper to taste

PREPARATION

■ *Melt the oil and butter together over a low heat.*
■ *Chop the onion fine, and soften it in the oil/butter mixture. Add the peas and cook them for a further 2 minutes.*
■ *Crumble the bouillon cube and add 3 cups/1¼ pt water. Bring the mixture to a boil.*
■ *As the broth boils, add the parsley and the rice. Cook for about 15 minutes until the rice has softened but remains firm, al dente.*
■ *Whisk in the grated Parmesan, season with the salt, and finish with a generous twist or three of black pepper.*

COOK'S TIPS

You could use frozen peas but the real point of this extraordinarily simple dish is the spiky flavor of fresh peas – so cook it only when the season is right. The texture, incidentally, is midway between soup and risotto, and requires a spoon.

Poached Egg in Broth

ZUPPA PAVESE

SERVES 6

Cooking time 10 minutes

Cooking time for the broth
3 hours

Oven temperature
375°F

INGREDIENTS

6 cups / 2½ pt light broth (*see*
Pastine in Brodo, p59)

6 slices good Italian bread

6 eggs

3 tbsp freshly grated
Parmesan

Salt and black pepper to taste

PREPARATION

■ *Bring the broth to a boil. As the broth is heating, toast the slices of bread to a light brown and set each in the bottom of an ovenproof soup dish.*
■ *Distribute the broth evenly among dishes.*
■ *Now carefully break an egg into each dish, over the slice of bread. Do not break the yolk.*
■ *Put the bowls into a preheated oven and bake for 10 minutes or until the eggs are just set.*
■ *Sprinkle each with the fresh Parmesan, season, and serve.*

COOK'S ASIDE

Another dish of bare-faced simplicity. The broth is clearly crucial, as is the absolute freshness of the cheese, about which a word: my esteemed colleague Georgio Raisa, a chef from the Veneto region, once tasted some of the pre-grated stuff they sell outside Italy. "*E di qual' albero, questo?*" "What tree does this come from?" he asked me. Try this dish with duck eggs as an experiment.

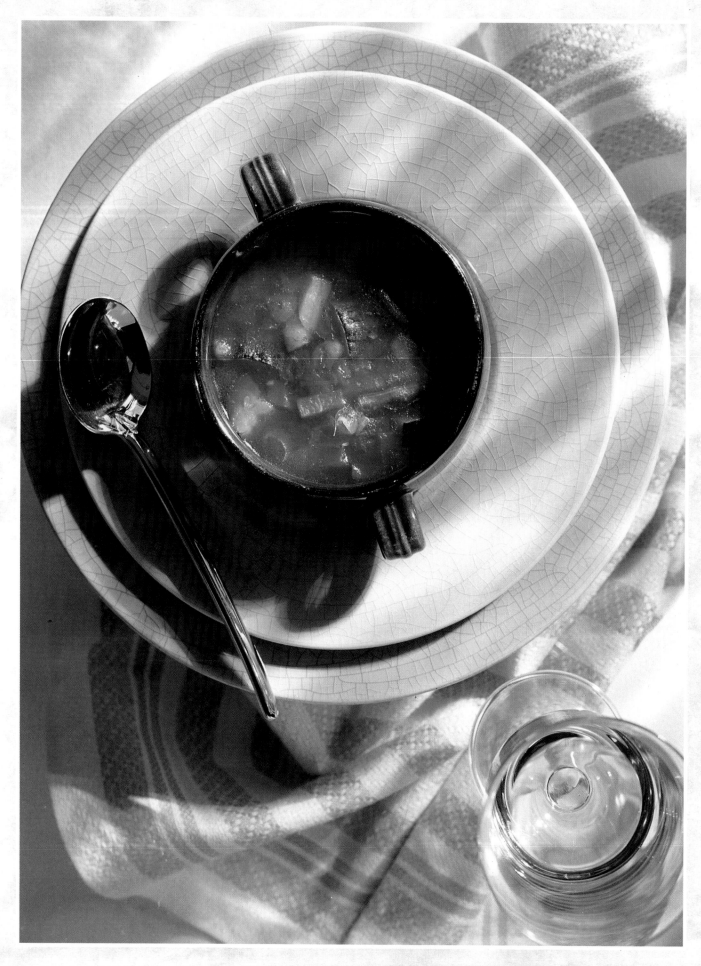

Vegetable Soup
MINESTRONE

SERVES 6 – 8

Cooking time about ½ hour

INGREDIENTS

4 tbsp olive oil

4 tbsp butter

3 large onions

2 cloves garlic

½ lb carrots

2 stalks celery

½ lb potatoes

½ lb cooked white beans (*see* Zuppa di Fagioli, p65)

¼ lb French beans

¼ lb zucchini

3 beef bouillon cubes (*see* Pastine in Brodo, p59)

¼ lb chopped fresh or tinned Italian tomatoes

¼ lb piece Parmesan cheese rind

Salt and pepper to taste

PREPARATION

■ *Melt the butter together with the oil over a medium heat. Chop the onions, garlic, potatoes, carrots, and celery fine, and add them, one vegetable at a time, to the oil and butter in a large pan. Cook each for 2 – 3 minutes, without browning.*

■ *Stir in the white and French beans. Chop the zucchini into larger pieces and add them to the mixture.*

■ *Crumble in the bouillon cubes and stir in 6 cups/2½ pt water. Stir in the tomatoes and add the whole cheese rind.*

■ *Cook the whole mixture together until you have a substantially thick soup – a consistency you must decide for yourself. Once your desire is satisfied in this matter, add water to maintain the consistency, if necessary, until the soup is thoroughly cooked – about 20 minutes. Season before serving and remember to remove the cheese rind.*

CHEF'S ASIDE

This is one version of *minestrone*. There are about as many as there are combinations of vegetables. Sometimes they contain pasta, sometimes rice, and sometimes the mixture is thick with lentils. There are just two serious rules: use a lot of vegetables and don't forget the cheese rind.

Garbanzo Bean Soup

ZUPPA DI CECI

Preparation time about
45 minutes

INGREDIENTS

4 cloves of garlic

½ tbsp dried rosemary leaves
(twice the quantity if
using fresh)

4 tbsp olive oil

5 oz canned Italian
tomatoes

1 lb tinned garbanzo beans,
drained and rinsed

1 chicken bouillon cube
(*see* Pastine in Brodo, p59)

Salt and pepper to taste

PREPARATION

■ *Peel and mince the garlic. If the rosemary is fresh, chop it very fine.*

■ *Heat the oil and sauté the garlic until it begins to brown. Add the rosemary and the tomatoes, roughly chopped, and lower the heat to a simmer when the ingredients come to a boil. Cook for 25 minutes or so.*

■ *When the tomatoes are cooked, add the garbanzo beans and cook for a further 5 minutes.*

■ *Stir in the bouillon cube and no more than 1¼ cups/½ pt water. Season with salt and pepper to taste, and serve.*

Bean Soup with Parsley, Garlic, and Chile
ZUPPA DI FAGIOLI ALL'ABRUZZESE

SERVES 4

Preparation time 1½ hours

Marinating time 12 hours

INGREDIENTS

¾ lb dried white kidney beans

4 cloves garlic

4 tbsp olive oil

4 tbsp tomato paste

2 tbsp fresh parsley, chopped fine

1 oz fresh chiles

Salt and pepper to taste

PREPARATION

▋ Soak the kidney beans in double their volume in water, in a warm place overnight.

▋ Ninety minutes before you wish to serve the soup – and that's a minimum – drain the beans, cover them with more water, and set them to boil over a low heat. Cook them for between 40 and 60 minutes, until they are tender. If you are using them immediately, let them stand in their cooking water. Otherwise, drain and store covered in the refrigerator.

▋ Peel and mince the garlic and soften it in the olive oil over a low heat. As it begins to color, drain away as much of the oil as you can and set it aside.

▋ Add the cooked beans, the tomato paste, the parsley, and no more than 1¼ cups/½ pt water. Bring the mixture to a boil then lower the heat to simmer.

▋ As the soup is cooking, slice and seed the fresh chiles and stew them very gently in the garlic-flavored olive oil until they are very soft. Pour the chili oil into a small serving bowl.

▋ Take half the quantity of the bean soup and liquidize it. When the consistency is completely smooth, combine the two parts of the soup.

▋ Check the seasoning. The soup is now ready to serve.

CHEF'S TIP

What, you ask, is the chili oil for? It is intended to be used as highly spiced condiment alongside the soup. The soup has a very thick, rich consistency and a soothing flavor. The chili oil provides a remarkable contrast.

Lentil Soup
ZUPPA DI LENTICCHE

SERVES 4 - 6
Cooking time about 1 hour
INGREDIENTS
2 tbsp olive oil
1 medium onion
1 stalk celery
2 slices bacon or *pançetta*
½ lb fresh or canned tomatoes
½ lb brown or green lentils
1 beef bouillon cube (*see* Pastine in Brodo, p59)
3 tbsp freshly grated Parmesan cheese
2 tbsp butter
Salt and freshly ground black pepper to taste

PREPARATION

■ In a good-size pan, heat the olive oil over a medium heat.

■ Slice the onion very fine, and soften it in the oil. Slice the celery fine, and add it to the onions when they are soft. Cook for a further 2 minutes or so.

■ As the celery is cooking, dice the bacon. Add it to the mixture.

■ Roughly chop the tomatoes and add them to the soup, together with the lentils.

■ Crumble in the bouillon cube and add 6 cups/2½ pt water. Bring to a boil on a high heat and then reduce to a simmer. You must cook the soup until the lentils are tender, up to 45 minutes. Test by tasting the soup occasionally. When the lentils are soft, season with the salt.

■ Off the heat, whisk in the butter and Parmesan. Pour the mixture into a suitable tureen, and generously coat the top with fresh black pepper.

Potato and Onion Soup

ZUPPA DI PATATE E CIPOLLE

SERVES 4 – 6

Cooking time about
30 minutes

INGREDIENTS

4 tbsp butter

2 tbsp olive oil

1½ lb onions

2 lb potatoes

1½ beef bouillon cubes
(*see* Pastine in Brodo, p59)

3 tbsp freshly grated
Parmesan cheese

Salt and freshly ground black
pepper to taste

PREPARATIONS

■ *Melt the oil and butter together over a high heat. Chop the onions fine, and cook them in the oil and butter until they turn light brown. Remove the pan from the heat.*

■ *Peel and dice the potatoes and boil them with the bouillon cubes and 3½ cups/1½ pts water until they are quite soft.*

■ *Now turn the potatoes and their water into the onion pan – which still contains the onions – and cook together for a further 10 minutes. As the mixture cooks, press the potatoes into the sides of the pan to loosen any caramelized onion residue.*

■ *Stir the cheese into the soup, season, and serve immediately.*

Red Lettuce and Rice Soup with Fresh Sage

ZUPPA DI RADICCHIO CON RISO E SALVIA

SERVES 4
Cooking time 30 minutes
INGREDIENTS
3 tbsp olive oil
1 small onion
2 cloves garlic
1 large head radicchio
1 chicken bouillon cube (*see* Pastine in Brodo, p59)
¼ lb risotto rice
1 heaping tbsp freshly grated Parmesan cheese
5 tbsp *fresh* sage, chopped fine – nothing else will do
Salt and pepper to taste

PREPARATIONS

■ *Heat the olive oil over a medium heat. Slice the onion fine, and sauté it until it softens. It must not color. Add the garlic, unchopped.*

■ *As the garlic and onions stew together, shred the radicchio fine. Add it to the pan and cook it until it softens completely – about 3 – 4 minutes.*

■ *Crumble in the bouillon cube and add 3½ cups/1½ pints water.*

■ *Add the rice and cook everything together until the rice is cooked but still firm – yes, al dente.*

■ *Whisk in the Parmesan and the finely chopped sage. Cook for another minute or so.*

■ *Season and serve.*

Mussel Soup

ZUPPA DI COZZE

SERVES 6
Cooking time 30 minutes
INGREDIENTS
4 tbsp olive oil
4 cloves garlic
2 tbsp fresh parsley, chopped fine
1 chile pepper, chopped fine
²/₃ cup / ¼ pt dry white wine
½ lb fresh tomatoes
2 lb fresh mussels

PREPARATIONS

■ In a pan large enough to hold everything, heat the olive oil. Mince the garlic (see Cook's Tips) and soften it in the oil.

■ Add the parsley and the chile. Turn the heat to high and pour in the white wine. The pan should sizzle.

■ Roughly chop the tomatoes and add to the pan. Lower the heat to a gentle simmer and cook the mixture, covered, for about 20 minutes.

■ As the mixture cooks, carefully scrub and debeard the mussels. Discard any that are open. After 20 minutes, add them to the pan and re-cover. The soup is ready when the mussels are open – about 5 minutes. (It is unlikely you will need salt.)

CHEF'S TIPS

As to mincing garlic, you are advised to avoid garlic presses. They are a complete waste of time. The professional minces the garlic clove firmly and progressively with the blade of a knife. This takes seconds and the knife can simply be wiped clean. Give the other thing – if you have one – to someone who doesn't cook.

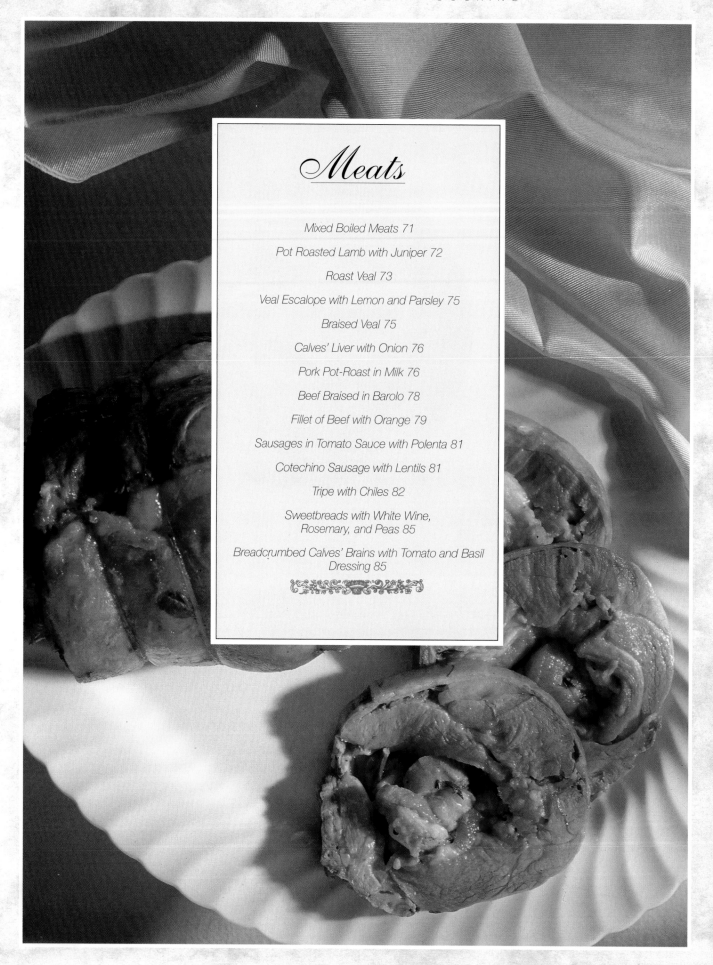

Meats

Mixed Boiled Meats 71

Pot Roasted Lamb with Juniper 72

Roast Veal 73

Veal Escalope with Lemon and Parsley 75

Braised Veal 75

Calves' Liver with Onion 76

Pork Pot-Roast in Milk 76

Beef Braised in Barolo 78

Fillet of Beef with Orange 79

Sausages in Tomato Sauce with Polenta 81

Cotechino Sausage with Lentils 81

Tripe with Chiles 82

Sweetbreads with White Wine,
Rosemary, and Peas 85

Breadcrumbed Calves' Brains with Tomato and Basil
Dressing 85

Mixed Boiled Meats

BOLLITO MISTO

SERVES 6
Preparation time 4 hours

INGREDIENTS

2 cloves garlic
1 medium onion
1 small fennel bulb
2 medium carrots
1 stalk celery
1 large beefsteak tomato
1½ lb beef tongue
2 lb beef brisket joint
1 medium chicken
1 cotechino sausage
Salt
2½ cups / 1 pt *bagnetto verde* (*see* Gamberoni al Bagnetto Verde)

PREPARATION

■ Beg, borrow, or steal a pan large enough to hold everything but the cotechino and the bagnetto verde.

■ Put all the vegetables in the pan, cover with water, and bring to a boil. Add the tongue and brisket, adjust the heat to a simmer, and add more water to cover if necessary. Skim occasionally.

■ After 2 hours, retrieve the tongue and remove the outer skin.

■ Pop it back in the pot.

■ After three hours, add the chicken. Cook the cotechino in another pan. Cook the bagnetto verde according to the recipe.

■ After 4 hours, your feast will be ready. Simply check the salt.

CHEF'S ASIDE

You should attempt to serve this dish all on one plate, with the meats carved and inter-leaved, and the by-now fragile vegetables arranged around them. It is an extraordinary party meal. As condiments go, the *bagnetto verde* is magnificent. But the dish is also served with mustard and, surprisingly, tomato ketchup. If you *were* looking for an excuse to have a party, this dish could be it.

Pot Roasted Lamb with Juniper
ARROSTO DI AGNELLO AL GINEPRO

SERVES 4
Cooking time 2½ hours
Oven temperature 350°F
INGREDIENTS
1 large shoulder of lamb (weighing about 2 lb)
¼ lb tritto (see Tritto)
1¼ cups / ½ pt dry white wine
2 good sprigs fresh rosemary
1 tbsp juniper berries
Salt and pepper to taste

PREPARATION

■ Heat, if available, a flameproof and ovenproof casserole. (Otherwise use a cookie tray and cover it with foil later.) Heat over a medium heat without oil.

■ When the pan is seriously hot, drop in the lamb shoulder. Singe it for a minute on one side then turn it and repeat. Remove it, and the pan, from the heat.

■ Now throw in the tritto, the white wine, the rosemary, and the juniper berries. Cover well and set to bake.

■ After 1 hour, check the liquid. Top it up to its original volume with water, if necessary.

■ Thirty minutes before serving, remove the lid. Season the juices with salt and pepper, and carve to serve. Could anything be simpler or more delightful?

Roast Veal

ARROSTO DI VITELLO

SERVES 6

Preparation time about 2½ hours

Oven temperature 350°F

INGREDIENTS

2 lb shoulder joint of veal

4 cloves garlic

2 sprigs fresh rosemary

1 shallow tsp peppercorns

2 tbsp olive oil

1¼ cups / ⅜ pt dry white wine

Salt to taste

PREPARATION

■ Bone the joint or ask your butcher to bone it for you. Cut along the plane of the joint so that you can open it more or less flat on the work surface.

■ Mince the garlic and bruise the rosemary. Rub both into the inner surface of the meat. Roughly crush peppercorns and sprinkle them on top. Roll the joint tight and secure it with loops of string. Ideally find a casserole dish with a cover that is both flameproof and ovenproof. Over a highish heat, heat the olive oil in the casserole and brown one side of the joint. Turn and brown the other. Cover and begin roasting.

■ The joint will take around 2 hours to cook. Halfway through, turn it over completely and add the white wine. This time, when it goes back in the oven, leave the lid ajar.

■ For the remaining hour, you will need to check the quantity of liquid every 20 minutes or so. If it drops below half, top it up with hot water.

■ To serve, let the joint rest for about 10 minutes before carving. Take the string off before you slice.

■ Do nothing to thicken the gravy beyond boiling it a little to reduce it. Start putting flour or gravy browning in there and someone will be sure to find out about it. Then you will become the laughing stock of all your right-thinking friends.

CHEF'S TIP

Very little could be more pleasant with this elegant roast than *spinaci conditi* (see Spinach with Oil, Lemon, and Pepper, p109) and some cool fried peppers. (see Fried Peppers with Tomato and Garlic, p108)

Veal Escalope with Lemon and Parsley

SCALLOPINE DI VITELLO AL LIMONE

SERVES 4
Preparation time 10 minutes
INGREDIENTS
2 tbsp olive oil
2 tbsp butter
1 lb veal for escalopes
Good ½ cup all-purpose flour
Juice of 2 lemons
4 tbsp fresh parsley, chopped fine
Salt and freshly ground black pepper

PREPARATION

▪ Cut the veal into 4 equal slices and into escalopes. (see Battening Meat Italian-Style, p15.)

▪ Melt the butter with the oil over a high heat. Dip each escalope into the flour, shake off the excess, and fry rapidly – about 1 minute each side. Set the escalopes aside in a warm place.

▪ Over a high heat, add the lemon juice to the pan juices with the parsley. Return the escalopes to the pan to warm them through – seconds only, for they are already cooked.

▪ Serve instantly, seasoned as you like them.

CHEF'S ASIDE

I know we have made one or two disparaging remarks about veal escalopes elsewhere. Nevertheless, they *are* eaten in Italy, but simply. This is one simple and excellent method.

Braised Veal

OSSO BUCO

SERVES 4
Cooking time 1½ hours
Oven temperature 350°F
INGREDIENTS
2 tbsp olive oil
8 oz *tritto* (see Tritto, p13)
4 veal cutlets (each weighing about 6 oz)
4 cloves garlic
1¼ cups / ½ pt dry white wine
¾ lb fresh or canned plum tomatoes, roughly chopped
2 tbsp green olives, pitted and halved
2 fresh bay leaves
1 tbsp fresh parsley, chopped fine
¼ oz thyme (fresh or dried)
Salt and freshly ground black pepper
2 tbsp fresh basil chopped fine

PREPARATION

▪ Preheat the oven. Over a medium heat on top of the stove, toss the oil and tritto together until the tritto softens – about 3 minutes.

▪ Increase the heat and add the veal steaks. Seal them well on either side. Now lift out the tritto vegetables and meat with a slotted spoon. Pour off most of the oil.

▪ Replace the ingredients and, over the same high heat, add the wine, the tomatoes, the olives, the bay leaves, the chopped parsley, and the thyme.

▪ Bring everything to a rolling boil, then cover well. Bake in the oven for about 1¼ hours.

▪ When the veal is cooked, lift it out and set it in a warm place. Boil the sauce hard to reduce its volume by about one-third. Season with the salt and pepper, throw in the fresh basil, pour over the meat, and serve.

Calves' Liver with Onion

FEGATO ALLA VENEZIANA

SERVES 4

Preparation time about 20 minutes

INGREDIENTS

2 tbsp olive oil

6 medium onions sliced very fine

2 leaves fresh sage

2 lb calves' liver

4 tbsp dry white wine

Salt and pepper to taste

PREPARATION

■ Heat the oil and add the onions. Allow them to cook until they are soft and medium brown in color. Roughly tear up the sage leaves and mix them into the onions when the latter are cooked.

■ Now remove the onions from the pan with a slotted spoon, and reserve them.

■ Slice the liver into thin strips and increase the heat to high. Toss in the liver when the pan is very hot. As soon as each piece is sealed take the liver from the pan (see Chef's Tips) and mix it with the onions.

■ Return the pan to a high heat and deglaze it with the white wine. When all has practically evaporated, return the onions and liver to the pan, reheat for seconds only, season, and serve immediately.

CHEF'S TIPS

You are not cooking the liver the first time out because it will continue to cook when it has left the pan. And in any event, this recipe gives you a second chance when you reheat it. But remember, sliced fine, calves' liver literally cooks in seconds. There is another thing the Italians frequently do with liver: *burro e salvia*. For that, clarify a large knob of butter, toss in the shredded fresh sage leaves, and fry the thin cut liver for 30 seconds a side and no more, in a very hot pan. Very good value, this part of the book: two recipes for the price of one!

Pork Pot-Roast in Milk

ARROSTO DI MAIALE AL LATTE

SERVES 6

Preparation time about 2 hours

Oven temperature 350°F

INGREDIENTS

4 tbsp butter

2 lb joint of boned pork, from the loin or leg

2½ cups / 1 pt milk

Salt and freshly ground black pepper to taste

8 fresh sage leaves

2 bay leaves

PREPARATION

■ Preheat the oven. Melt the butter over a medium heat on top of the stove in the dish you are going to use for the pork – a casserole dish with a lid if you have one.

■ When the butter begins to foam, add the joint and brown in on all sides.

■ Now slowly pour in the milk. The stream should be slow enough to boil as soon as it hits the dish. Season with the salt and pepper and throw in the sage and bay leaves.

■ Loosely cover the dish – with its own lid or with baking foil, if you're using a roasting tray – and consign it to the oven department.

■ Turn the joint completely halfway through cooking time – after about 1 hour. Top up the milk at that point if the level is below half.

■ When the joint is cooked, let it stand for 10 minutes or so before carving. This gives you time to deal with the juices.

■ If the milk is still creamy and pale, boil it down until it begins to caramalize. If not, immediately add half a cup or so of water to the dish and de-glaze. (Don't be tempted to use wine or broth here. What we're after is the pure flavor of the pan juices, milk and herbs.)

■ Carve the meat, spoon the sauce over it, and serve.

Beef Braised in Barolo

MANZO AL BAROLO

SERVES 6

SERVES 6

Preparation time 3 hours

Oven temperature
350°F

INGREDIENTS

2 tbsp olive oil

1 beef joint of about 2 lb

¼ lb *tritto* (see Tritto, p13)

1¼ cups / ½ pt Barolo
or other dry red wine

1¼ cups / ½ pt broth
(use beef bouillon cube or *see*
Pastine in Brodo, p59)

2 oz fresh or canned plum
tomatoes

¼ oz each of thyme and
marjoram

Salt to taste

PREPARATION

■ *Preheat the oven. Heat the oil over a medium heat on top of the above and brown the joint of beef. Seal it in every possible place then set it aside.*

■ *Now add the tritto to the beef pan and cook it until soft 3 – 4 minutes.*

■ *Transfer the beef to a casserole a littler larger than the beef itself. Retrieve the tritto with a slotted spoon – without the oil. Spread it over and around the beef. Pour in the wine, the broth, and the tomatoes; add the herbs.*

■ *Put the beef in the oven, covered with a well-fitting lid. Turn the joint completely over at halfway through.*

■ *To serve, carve the joint and spoon the sauce over, checking for salt before you do.*

■ *Watch two things: the rate of evaporation of the liquid in the pot, which you may have to top up with water, and the thickness of the final gravy. Thicken it by reducing, if you so desire. In this case, salt afterwards and not before.*

CHEF'S ANECDOTE

Barolo is a superb wine, arguably Italy's best red. It comes from Piedmont, also the home of Signora Olga Bernardi, to whom this book is substantially dedicated.

I had a whole bottle to myself one year. It was a '74 and I was to drink it on a sunny terrace high in the mountains on the first day of April.

The wine arrived and it was magnificent. The main course arrived too – an escalope Milanese. This was not so magnificent. In fact, it was a stiff piece of cardboard, heavily breadcrumbed. They have April Fool's Day in Italy too.

Fillet of Beef with Orange

FILLETTO ALL' ARANCIA

SERVES 4

Cooking time 20 minutes

INGREDIENTS

1 tbsp olive oil

4 fillet steaks (each weighing about 6 oz)

4 tbsp Marsala

4 tbsp red wine

2 Seville oranges

Salt and a generous amount of coarsely ground black pepper

PREPARATION

■ Heat the oil in as heavy a skillet as you have. Brown the steaks for a minute on each side. Retrieve them from the pan and set them aside in a very warm place. (An oven at 275°F would do.) Over a very high heat, add the Marsala and red wine to deglaze the pan.

■ Lower the heat, zest the oranges, and add both juice and zest to the pan.
■ If you prefer your meat medium, return the steaks to the pan and reheat them as the juices reduce. For rare steaks, cook the wine and juice down to a consistency of light syrup before you return the meat.
■ To serve, pour the juices over each steak. Arrange the zest in an attractive way on top of the meat. Sprinkle with salt and a generous amount of black pepper before eating.

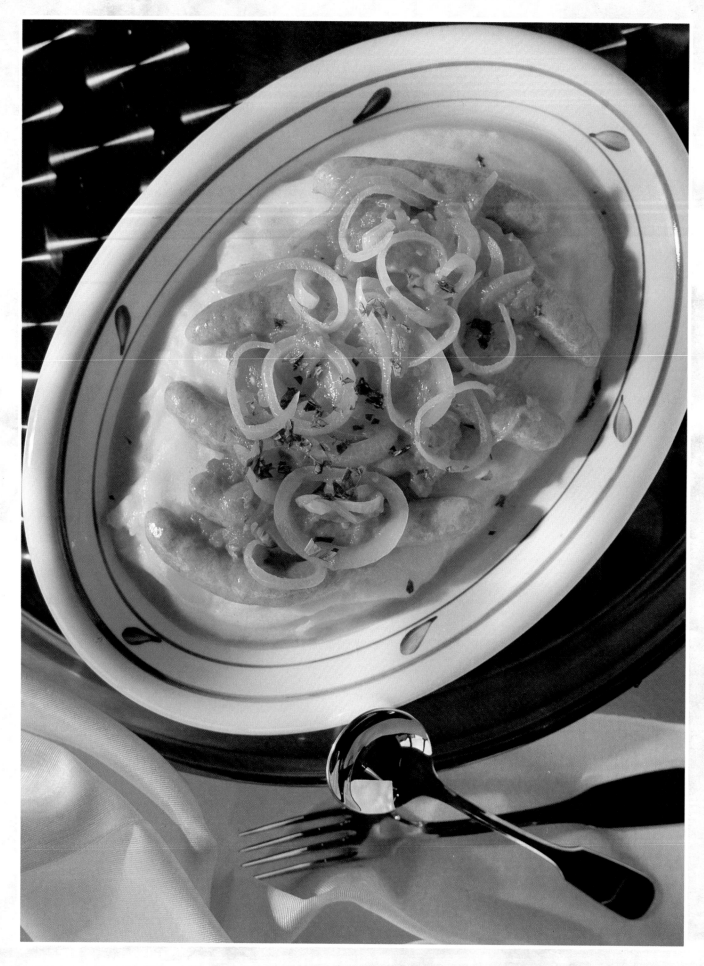

Sausages in Tomato Sauce with Polenta

SALSICCIE CON POLENTA

SERVES 6

Cooking time 35 minutes

INGREDIENTS

4 tbsp olive oil

4 cloves garlic

1 medium onion, sliced fine

1 lb fresh or canned
plum tomatoes

²⁄₃ cup / ¼ pt dry white wine

1 chile

1½ lb uncooked
continental-style sausage

¾ lb polenta (*see* How To
Make Polenta)

2 tbsp fresh basil,
chopped fine

Salt and freshly ground black
pepper to taste

PREPARATION

▮ *Heat the oil in a sturdy pan. Add the garlic and the finely sliced onion. As the onions are softening, roughly chop the tomatoes. Add them when the onion is just beginning to brown, and turn the heat to medium high.*

▮ *Add the white wine and the chile, and bring the sauce to a boil. Turn to a low simmer, add the sausages, and cover the pot.*

▮ *As the sausages are braising, cook the polenta as in the recipe.*

▮ *Sausages and polenta will be ready together. Just before you serve the one spooned generously over the other, add the finely chopped basil to the sausages and check the seasoning. More pepper than salt is my guess.*

Cotechino Sausages with Lentil

COTECHINO CON LE LENTICHE

SERVES 6

Pre-preparation time
4 – 8 hours

Preparation time 2 – 3 hours

INGREDIENTS

1 cotechino sausage (*see*
Chef's Tips)

2 tbsp olive oil

4 cloves garlic

1 medium onion, roughly
chopped

4 tbsp tomato paste

²⁄₃ cup / ¼ pt red wine

2 tbsp fresh sage

½ lb green lentils

Salt and pepper to taste

PREPARATION

▮ *Soak the sausage in cold water for at least 4 hours or overnight. About 3 hours away from eating set the sausage to boil, whole and unpricked, in plenty of water – at least 13 cups/5 pt – and start from cold. Simmer until tender – about 2½ hours.*

▮ *With 1 hour to go, heat the olive oil to near smoking in a heavy pan. Throw in the garlic, unchopped, and the onion.*

▮ *Cook the onion hard until it begins to brown around the edges; and then drop the heat to low. While the pan is still hot, add the tomato paste, red wine, and the sage, and stir well. Let the sage infuse in the liquids for 2–3 minutes. Add the lentils and again stir well.*

▮ *Pour in water to cover the lentils by 1-in and cook on a low simmer until tender, about 40 minutes. Keep checking the water content. Add more to cover the lentils if you have to.*

▮ *When the lentils are tender, let them stand to absorb whatever water remains in the pot. They should be coated with a thick, moist sheen, but should not be swimming. If there is too much liquid, increase the heat and boil it off. Season to taste.*

▮ *Remove the cotechino from its broth when cooked. Slice and serve it on top of the lentils.*

CHEF'S TIPS

You will have to find an ethnic butcher for the cotechino. On no account use already-cooked salami.

Tripe with Chiles

TRIPPA CON PEPERONCINI

SERVES 6
Cooking time about 2 hours
INGREDIENTS
2 lb honeycomb tripe (*see* Chef's Tips)
4 tbsp olive oil
4 cloves garlic, chopped
1 medium onion, chopped
1 lb fresh or canned plum tomatoes, roughly chopped
⅔ cup / ¼ pt dry white wine
1 oz dried ceps, washed and dried
4 chile peppers
1 sprig fresh rosemary
2 anchovy fillets
Salt and pepper to taste

PREPARATION

■ *Bring 13 cups/5 pt water to a boil and plunge the tripe into it. Boil it for 30 minutes.*

■ *As the tripe is cooking, heat the oil, soften the garlic and onions together in it, and add the tomatoes, the wine, the ceps, and ⅔ cup/¼ pt water. Bring everything to a boil.*

■ *As the sauce is warming, slice and deseed 2 chiles. Add all chile pieces, the rosemary, and the anchovy fillets to the sauce. When it boils, turn the heat to a very low simmer and cover.*

■ *When the tripe has boiled for 30 minutes, remove it and slice very fine. Add it to the sauce and cook until tender enough to cut with a fork – about 1 hour. Season and serve.*

CHEF'S DIGRESSION

My childhood memories of tripe in the North of England are gloomy in the extreme. I seem to recall a pale-colored, folding substance, in texture a cross between an army blanket and a retired sponge, in flavor the very essence of a large bottle of malt vinegar. Even in the days before central heating for us sons of toil, this delicacy was always served well below room temperature.

However, such faith do I place in the Signora Olga Bernardi, the Queen of Capanna Kind, Empress of Sportinia and purveyor of matrimonial advice to myself (seated in the dining room), and the characters of Dallas (inside the TV set) that when she offered me tripe for lunch, I accepted gratefully. Not that I had any choice – she doesn't give you one.

It was terrific, of course. Needless to say, she also did what Elizabeth David characters are always doing in cookery books – throwing a little something she just happened to find in the garden. In this case it was ceps – *funghi porcini* which she had picked herself in the summer and preserved in oil. You can buy the same things, preserved the same way, in Italian supermarkets. They're much more expensive than the dried, but they are certainly worth considering.

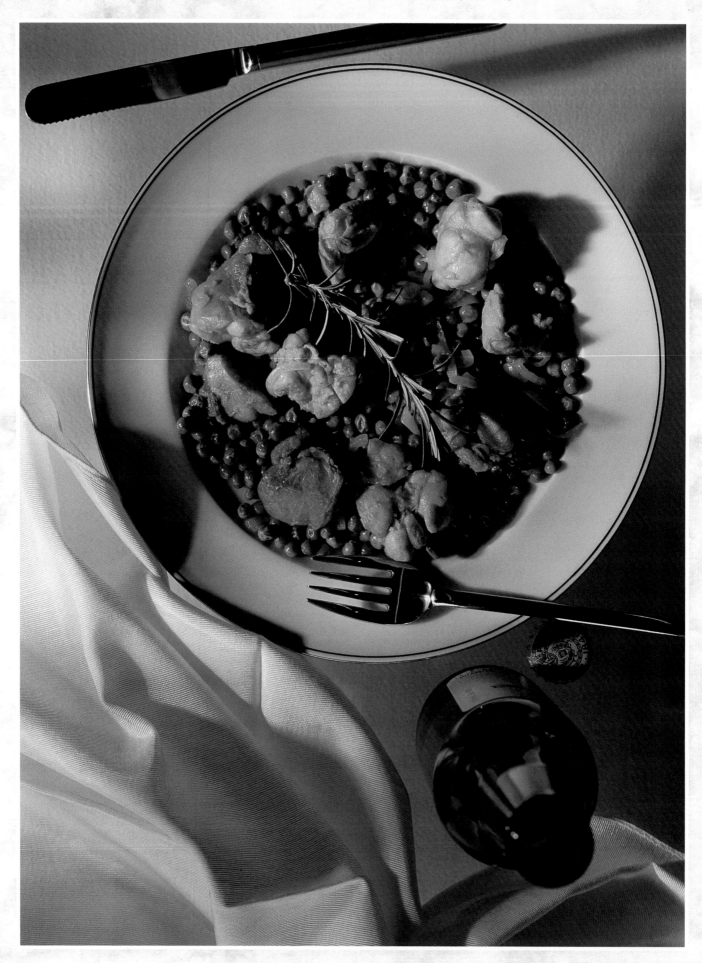

Sweetbreads with White Wine, Rosemary, and Peas

ANIMELLE CON PISELLI E ROSEMARINO

SERVES 4 – 6
Preparation time about 40 minutes

INGREDIENTS
1 carrot, roughly chopped
1 stalk celery, roughly chopped
2 small onions
½ lemon
1½ lb sweetbreads (see Chef's Tips)
5 tbsp olive oil
1¼ cups / ½ pt dry white wine
¾ lb shelled peas, fresh or frozen
1 good sprig fresh rosemary
1 chile pepper
Salt and freshly ground black pepper to taste

PREPARATION

■ Bring 8½ cups/3½ pt water to a boil and add the roughly chopped carrot and celery, 1 onion, and the half lemon.

■ Poach the sweetbreads in the court bouillon for five minutes.

■ Remove the sweetbreads. You will now clearly see the membrane around them. Carefully remove as much of this as you can and then set the sweetbreads aside.

■ Heat the olive oil over a medium heat. Finely slice the other onion and sauté it in the oil. Add the breads, sliced into 1-in chunks and brown them over a medium heat with the onions for about 3–4 minutes. Add the white wine, the peas – if using fresh ones, the rosemary, and the whole chile. Cover the pot and poach the breads for 15–20 minutes.

■ Remove the sweetbreads and set them aside.

■ Over a very high heat, reduce the cooking liquors until there will be just enough left to glaze the sweetbreads. Return them to the pan, with the frozen peas, if used. Season and serve as soon as everything is hot.

CHEF'S TIP
We are not going to tell you what sweetbreads are. Suffice to say they are not what you think, if that is what you thought.

Breadcrumbed Calves' Brains with Tomato and Basil Dressing

CERVELLA FRITTA CON POMODORI FRESCHI

SERVES 6
Preparation time 30 minutes

INGREDIENTS
2 calves' brains
Juice of lemon
1 medium carrot
½ medium fennel bulb
1 small onion
4 tbsp vinegar
¾ cup / 6 fl oz olive oil
½ lb fresh plum tomatoes
1 oz fresh basil
Salt and freshly ground black pepper to taste
3 cups fine fresh bread crumbs
1½ tbsp freshly grated Parmesan cheese
2 eggs

PREPARATION

■ Soak the calves' brains in cold water and lemon juice.

■ Chop the carrot, fennel, and onion roughly, bring 3¾ cups / 1¾ pt water to a boil, and add the vegetables and the vinegar.

■ Drain the brains, peel off any obvious membranous parts, and drop them into the boiling water. Poach at a low simmer for 15 minutes.

■ As the brains are cooking, divide the oil between two bowls. Skin the tomatoes, chop them roughly, and chop the basil fine. Mix the tomatoes, basil, salt, and pepper in one bowl of oil, and transfer to a serving dish.

■ Drain the brains, pat them dry, and set them aside in the refrigerator or another cool place.

■ Mix the bread crumbs and the cheese in a shallow dish. Break eggs and beat them in a shallow bowl.

■ Retrieve the brains from the cool place. Slice them widthwise into ½-in rounds, dip each in the egg, shake off any excess, then press each side firmly into the crumbs.

■ Fry them in the remaining olive oil over medium heat until the crumbs form a crisp crust. Serve with the tomato and basil sauce underneath.

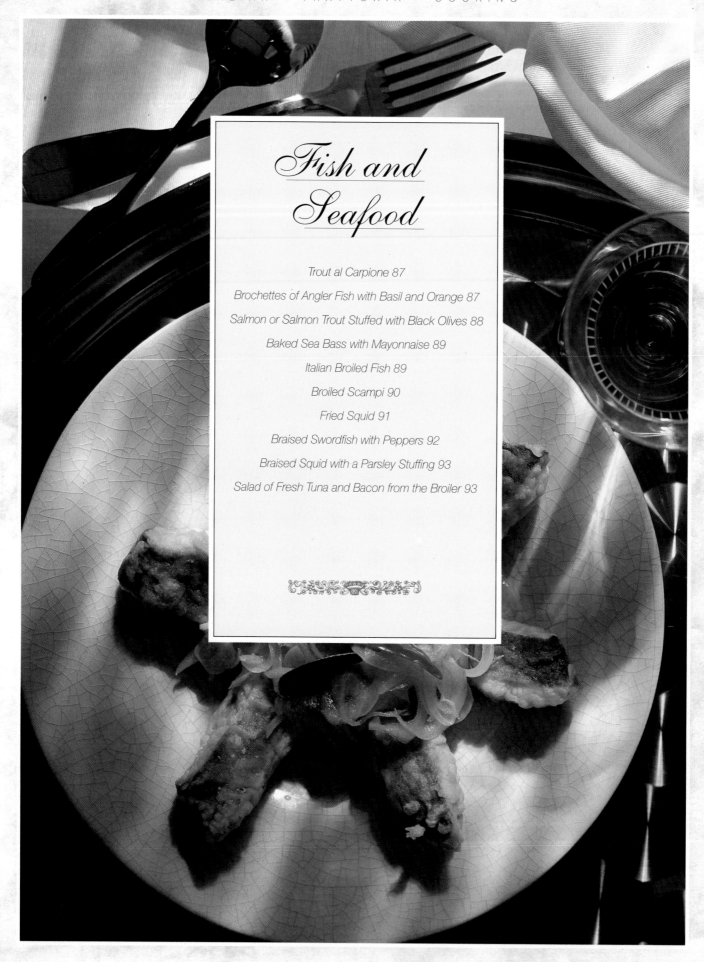

Fish and Seafood

Trout al Carpione 87

Brochettes of Angler Fish with Basil and Orange 87

Salmon or Salmon Trout Stuffed with Black Olives 88

Baked Sea Bass with Mayonnaise 89

Italian Broiled Fish 89

Broiled Scampi 90

Fried Squid 91

Braised Swordfish with Peppers 92

Braised Squid with a Parsley Stuffing 93

Salad of Fresh Tuna and Bacon from the Broiler 93

Trout al Carpione

TROTA AL CARPIONE

SERVES 6
Preparation time about 45 minutes

INGREDIENTS

6 medium rainbow trout or 1 salmon trout (about 3.25 lb)

1 egg

1¼ cup / ½ pt olive oil

1 cup / 4 oz all-purpose flour

1 large onion

4 cloves garlic

⅔ cup / ¼ pt dry white wine

2 tbsp vinegar

2 tbsp sugar

2 large sprigs rosemary

4 fresh bay leaves

1 chile pepper

Salt to taste

PREPARATION

■ Clean and dry the fish. If you are using salmon trout, cut it into slices about ⅓ in thick.

■ Beat the egg and mix with its own volume of water.

■ Heat about one-third of the oil to a medium heat, dip the whole fish or slices in the egg/water mixture, and then roll in the flour. Fry gently until cooked – the whole trout 8 minutes per side, the slices 4–5. When cooking fish in this way turn it once only.

■ Carefully remove the fish when it is cooked and arrange it prettily on a serving dish.

■ Now proceed as for Eggplants al Carpione. Set the rest of the olive oil on a medium heat. Slice the onion very fine and stew it in the oil. (Stew, not fry!) Add the garlic and cook both together until the onion is completely soft. Neither must brown.

■ Add the wine, vinegar, sugar, rosemary, bay leaves, and the whole chile. Bring everything to a boil and season. Pour the mixture over the fish and serve – warm, cool, or chilled.

Brochettes of Angler Fish with Basil and Orange

SPIEDINI DI CODA DI ROSPO ALL' ARANCIA

SERVES 4
Preparation time 15 minutes
Marinating time 2 hours

INGREDIENTS

2 lb angler fish

2 oranges

⅔ cup / ¼ pt olive oil

1 tbsp fresh basil, chopped fine

½ cup fresh bread crumbs

Salt and freshly grated black pepper

PREPARATION

■ Skin the angler fish and dice it into 2-in square chunks.

■ Squeeze the juices from the oranges. Cut the skins into chunks about the size of the fish pieces and reserve. Combine the olive oil, the orange juice, and the basil.

■ Add the fish to the marinade and scatter with the pieces of orange zest. Marinate for up to 2 hours.

■ Preheat the broiler to its maximum heat. Thread the fish onto skewers, alternating the pieces whenever you can with pieces of orange peel.

■ Brush liberally with the marinade once more. Sprinkle the side you are broiling first with half the bread crumbs. Broil for 6 – 7 minutes. Turn, bread crumb the other side, and broil again. Remove the brochettes to a serving platter.

■ Combine any pan juices with what remains of the marinade. Bring to a rapid boil, season, and pour over the fish.

Salmon or Salmon Trout Stuffed with Black Olives

SALMONE RIPIENO ALLA PIEMONTESE

Preparation time 50 minutes

Oven temperature
350°F

INGREDIENTS

1 small salmon or large salmon
trout (about 4½ lb)

½ lb fresh or canned
plum tomatoes

4 tbsp olive oil

4 cloves garlic

2 sprigs *fresh* rosemary

6 anchovy fillets

1 oz black olives

2 tbsp white wine vinegar

4 tbsp dry white wine

2 tbsp brandy

Salt and freshly ground black
pepper to taste

PREPARATION

■ *Preheat the oven. Clean and de-scale the fish (see Chef's Tips for Baked Sea Bass.)*
■ *Roughly chop the tomatoes and spread them out on a large sheet of foil.*
■ *Mix the olive oil with the chopped tomatoes and lay the fish on top.*
■ *Crush the garlic and smear the inside of the fish with it; lay the sprigs of rosemary and the anchovy fillets at equal intervals inside the cavity. Chop the olives very fine and sprinkle half inside, half outside.*
■ *Combine the wine vinegar and brandy and pour over the fish, then lift the sides of the foil and seal the fish carefully.*
■ *Bake the fish for 35 minutes.*
■ *Lift the fish from the foil with a long spatula when it is cooked. Take care when transferring it so that it does not break, and set it on a serving dish.*
■ *Pour all the juices from the foil into a pan and bring them to a rapid boil. Season with salt and pepper, pour over the fish, and consume.*

Baked Sea Bass with Mayonnaise

BRANZINO AL CARTOCCIO CON MAIONESE

SERVES 6
Preparation time 35 minutes
Standing time 3 – 4 hours
Oven temperature 350°F

INGREDIENTS
1 sea bass (about 3½ lb)
2 large onions
4 tbsp olive oil
2 cloves garlic
2 sprigs rosemary
2 tbsp fresh parsley, chopped fine
2 tbsp finely chopped fresh basil
Juice of 1 lemon
4 tbsp dry white wine
Salt and freshly ground black pepper
2½ cups / 1 pt mayonnaise (see Mayonnaise)

PREPARATION

■ *Preheat the oven. Clean and de-scale the fish (see Chef's Tips.)*

■ *Very finely slice the onion and make a fish-shaped bed of it on a large piece of foil. Pour the olive oil over it and lay the fish on top.*

■ *Now crush the garlic and smear along the inside of the fish. Lay the sprigs of rosemary in there too. Chop the parsley and basil fine, mix with the lemon juice, and similarly anoint the inside of the fish.*

■ *Raise the edges of the foil, pour over the white wine, and season. Seal the parcel carefully, making sure there are no holes or tears.*

■ *Set the parcel in an ample-size dish and bake for 30 minutes. When ready, remove from the oven, but do not unseal until the parcel is completely cool.*

■ *In the meantime, make the mayonnaise.*

■ *About 45 minutes before eating, remove the fish from its wrapper and collect all the juices into a small saucepan. Boil them down and cool; then add them to the mayonnaise.*

■ *Decorate the fish with onions on which it lay and serve.*

CHEF'S TIPS

De-scaling can be a messy process. Flakes fly everywhere. If you can, therefore, hold the fish underwater as you scrape. Hold the knife at right angles to the fish and scrape from tail to head to dislodge the scales. (An even cleaner method is to ask the fishmerchant.)

It has been pointed out to me that there may be some people in the world unaware that cleaning a fish is not like cleaning a car: that is, you don't just swab it down with water and a sponge until the outside looks shiny! To clean a fish, make a single cut from the waste pipe to the mouth. Push your hand up into the head, close your fingers firmly, and pull. Everything from the lungs down will come away, if not cleanly. Wash away all traces of blood, and proceed.

Italian Broiled Fish

PESCE ALLA GRIGLIA

SERVES 4
Preparation time 15 minutes
Standing time 2 hours

INGREDIENTS
6 whole fish (about 12 oz each)
⅔ cup / ¼ pt olive oil
Juice of 1 lemon
Freshly grated black pepper
2 tbsp fresh oregano
1 tbsp very fine bread crumbs
Rock salt to taste

PREPARATION

■ *Clean, dry and de-scale the fish, if necessary (see Chef's Tips for Baked Sea Bass). Combine the oil and lemon juice, and coat the fish thoroughly.*

■ *Combine the black pepper, oregano, bread crumbs, and salt and rub into the fish. Leave to stand prepared for about 2 hours.*

■ *Heat the broiler to maximum heat and cook the fish, turning only once.*

CHEF'S TIP

Any fish will do, but sea fish are recommended. The crucial quality is absolute *freshness*. Use mackerel only if you caught it yourself.

Broiled Scampi

SCAMPI AI FERRI

SERVES 4

Preparation time 10 minutes

INGREDIENTS

24 large scampi
(see Chef's Tips)

⅔ cup / ¼ pt olive oil

Juice of 1 lemon

3 tbsp freshly grated
Parmesan cheese

½ cup fresh bread crumbs

Rock salt

PREPARATION

■ Cut the fish in half lengthwise, leaving a thin strip of shell at the back so the 2 pieces remain just attached.
■ Combine half the oil and the lemon juice and brush each fish with the mixture. Combine the cheese and the bread crumbs, and sprinkle over the exposed flesh. Sprinkle the fish with the remaining oil and dot with rock salt.
■ Preheat the broiler to maximum and broil until the cheese forms a light brown crust (see Chef's Tips). Serve instantly.

CHEF'S TIPS

Scampi is the Italian for langoustine, which is the French for Dublin Bay Prawn. The creatures are the same size as large Mediterranean prawns, but are distinguished from them by their prominent, lobster-like claws. They can be bought live or frozen uncooked. On no account buy cooked ones: it does not improve the flavor to cook fish twice. As to the light brown crust, there is one way of telling when these fish are ready. You will immediately detect a rich, broiled fish smell. Cooking time is very short, by the way. How short depends on the heat of your broiler.

Fried Squid

CALAMARI FRITTI

Preparation time about
15 minutes

INGREDIENTS

Scant 4½ lb small squid

1½ cups all-purpose flour

Salt and freshly grated
black pepper

2½ cups / 1 pt vegetable
oil (see Chef's Tips)

3 lemons

PREPARATION

■ *Clean the squid (see Chef's Tips in Braised Squid). Slice the body sacs into rings – 5 or 6 per body for small animals.*

■ *Heat the oil until it is almost smoking. Here you must use your imagination a little. You are going to fry the squid in batches small enough not to produce a serious drop in the oil temperature. If any doubt, start with just 2 or 3 and slowly work up.*

■ *Dip the squid in the flour, one batch at a time so the coating does not become soggy, shake off the excess, and fry until light brown – about 30 – 40 seconds if the temperature is right. Set each batch to drain on paper towels.*

■ *Check for salt once more when all is cooked and serve very hot, with the lemon cut in wedges.*

Braised Swordfish with Peppers

PESCE ESPADA BRASATO CON PEPERONI

SERVES 4
Preparation time 30 minutes
INGREDIENTS
4 swordfish steaks (about 6 oz each)
4 tbsp olive oil
4 cloves garlic
1 medium onion, roughly chopped
1 medium red bell pepper
¼ lb fresh or canned plum tomatoes, roughly chopped
1 chile pepper
⅔ cup / ¼ pt dry white wine
Salt and pepper to taste

PREPARATION

■ Wash and thoroughly dry the steaks. Heat the oil over a high heat and seal each steak on each side.

■ Remove the fish from the pan and reserve it. Turn down the heat to medium and add the whole cloves of garlic and the onions.

■ Turn the heat once more to high and cook the onions until the edges begin to brown. Reduce the heat to a gentle simmer and cook on until the onions and garlic are softened. In the meantime, deseed and finely slice the peppers.

■ When the onions are soft, add the peppers and cook until they begin to soften – about 5 minutes. Add the tomatoes, the whole chile and the wine. Bring to a fierce boil, then add the fish. Turn the heat to a low simmer and cover the pan, sit down (and have a glass of wine).

■ Simmer until the fish is very tender, about 15 minutes.

■ Remove the fish from the pan and set it aside in a warm place. Boil up the pan juices very briskly, until they are reduced to a thick, creamy mixture. Season, pour around the fish, and serve.

Braised Squid with a Parsley Stuffing
CALAMARI RIPIENI ALLA MARINARA

SERVES 6
Preparation time 45 minutes
INGREDIENTS
12 squid (about 3¼ in long)
2 tbsp finely chopped fresh parsley
2 cloves garlic, minced
3 tbsp freshly grated Parmesan cheese
½ cup fresh bread crumbs
2 anchovy fillets
1 egg
6 tbsp olive oil
½ lb fresh or canned plum tomatoes
⅔ cup / ¼ pt dry white wine
1 chile pepper
Salt to taste

PREPARATION

■ *Clean the squid and finely chop the tentacles (see Chef's Tips).*

■ *Combine the parsley, the garlic, and bread crumbs. Mash and mix in the anchovy fillets.*

■ *Beat the egg and mix it with the bread mixture. Add about half the oil and the tentacles of the squid. Now push the mixture into the squid bodies, stopping about two-thirds of the way down. (The squid will shrink as it cooks and thus push the stuffing down to the end.)*

■ *Heat the rest of the oil in a pan large enough to hold all the fish in one layer. Roughly chop the tomatoes and add them to the oil with the wine and the whole chile.*

■ *Bring the tomatoes and wine to a boil, then turn the heat to a very low simmer. Add the squid and seal the pan tightly. Cook for about 30 minutes, until a fork will easily pierce the squid. Season the sauce and wait, if you like – this dish may be served hot, cold, or in between.*

CHEF'S TIPS

Cleaning squid: seize the tentacles and pull – the head and digestive businesses will follow them easily out of the tube-like outer body. Run your finger down the body to squeeze out any residue.

You will notice the tip of something that looks like a piece of transparent cellulose protruding from the body sac. This is the creature's extraordinary backbone. Thumb and forefinger will tease it out quite easily. But don't snap it: it will become difficult to reach.

Cut the tentacles away just above the point they join. Discard the rest.

Salad of Fresh Tuna and Bacon from the Broiler
INSALATA DI TONNO PASSATO ALLA G'RIGLIA

SERVES 4
Preparation time 20 minutes
Marinating time 2 hours
INGREDIENTS
2 lb fresh tuna
1 lb bacon or *pancetta*
4 tbsp fresh oregano
⅔ cup / ¼ pt olive oil
Juice of 1 lemon
2 cloves garlic, well minced
Salt and freshly ground black pepper to taste
1½ tbsp freshly grated Parmesan cheese

PREPARATION

■ *Dice the tuna into thumb-size chunks. Lay the pancetta out in flat strips and spread it with the oregano, very finely chopped.*

■ *Lay a piece of tuna at the start of each bacon strip, roll in the bacon and pin with a toothpick. Continue thus down each strip of bacon until all the tuna is wrapped.*

■ *Combine the olive oil and lemon juice and add to it the garlic. Marinate the pinned pieces of tuna and bacon in the mixture for about 2 hours.*

■ *Preheat the broiler to its highest setting. Thread the bacon and fish chunks on to skewers. Imagine the skewers have 4 faces. Broil each face for 2 minutes – a quarter turn 4 times.*

■ *Detach the fish from the skewers when cooked, then separate the fish and bacon. Finely chop the bacon pieces.*

■ *Dress the fish in the marinade, season, and sprinkle over the bacon and Parmesan. Serve warmish.*

CHEF'S TIP

This dish is wonderful with the bitter taste of radicchio. Shred two heads and serve the salad on top.

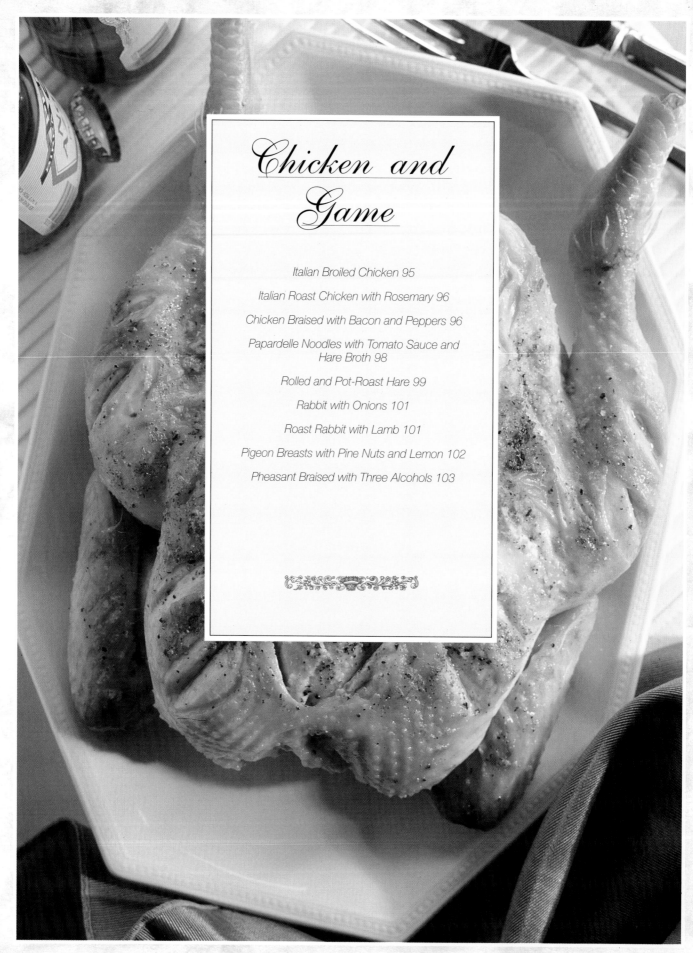

Chicken and Game

Italian Broiled Chicken 95

Italian Roast Chicken with Rosemary 96

Chicken Braised with Bacon and Peppers 96

Papardelle Noodles with Tomato Sauce and
Hare Broth 98

Rolled and Pot-Roast Hare 99

Rabbit with Onions 101

Roast Rabbit with Lamb 101

Pigeon Breasts with Pine Nuts and Lemon 102

Pheasant Braised with Three Alcohols 103

Italian Broiled Chicken

POLLO ALLA DIAVOLA

SERVES 4
Preparation time 30 minutes
Marinating time 2 hours
INGREDIENTS
1 roasting chicken (weighing about 2½ – 3 lb)
Juice of two lemons
⅔ cup / ¼ pt olive oil
1 heaped tbsp peppercorns
Rock salt to taste

PREPARATION

■ *Take a large pair of scissors to the chicken's backbone and cut it out. Lay the bird breast side up on your work-top and press down onto the breast to flatten it. Now cut diagonal slashes across the breasts and thighs.*

■ *Set the chicken in a dish and pour over it the lemon juice and olive oil. Very roughly crush the peppercorns and sprinkle them over the chicken. Let it marinate for about two hours.*

■ *Preheat the broiler. It should be as hot as possible.*

■ *After marinating, sprinkle the chicken breasts liberally with the rock salt. Broil until the breasts turn light brown. Turn the chicken over. Pour some of the marinade into the cavity and broil for a further 10 minutes.*

■ *Turn once more, baste with the marinade (scoop up the juices from the broiler pan, too), and remove when the whole bird is a tempting mid-brown.*

Italian Roast Chicken with Rosemary

POLLO ARROSTO CON ROSMARINO

SERVES 4
Preparation time 1 hour or so
Oven temperature 375°F

INGREDIENTS
1 roasting chicken (about 2½ – 3 lb)
4 cloves garlic
4 good sprigs fresh rosemary
4 oz *tritto* (see Tritto, p13)
4 tbsp olive oil
4 tbsp dry white wine
Salt to taste

PREPARATION

■ Preheat the oven. Put the chicken in a roasting tin, crush the garlic roughly and smear it around the cavity of the chicken, and put 2 sprigs of rosemary inside with it, then chop the remainder, and sprinkle it over and around the bird with tritto and oil. Commit the whole ensemble to the oven.

■ The chicken will be cooked in an hour or so, but baste it thoroughly with the pan juices every 15 minutes.

■ When cooking is complete, let the bird rest for 5 minutes or so. Skim the oil off the pan juices and set the dish over a very high heat. Add the wine and bring everything to a rapid boil. Season, pour over the chicken, and serve.

Chicken Braised with Bacon and Red Peppers

POLLO CON PEPERONI E PANCETTA

SERVES 4
Preparation time 45 minutes

INGREDIENTS
1 roasting chicken (about 2½ – 3 lb)
4 tbsp olive oil
4 red bell peppers
4 cloves garlic
4 chile peppers
½ lb bacon or *pancetta*
Salt to taste

PREPARATION

■ Joint the chicken into 4 pieces. Heat the oil in your heaviest casserole – one with a good lid – and thoroughly brown the chicken pieces. Remove them from the heat.

■ Deseed the bell peppers and slice into fine strips. Cook until soft in the chicken oil – about 10 minutes. Return the chicken pieces to the pan, smothering them with the peppers.

■ Add the whole garlic and the whole chiles. Lay the strips of bacon over everything, cover the pan, and cook at a very low heat until the chicken is tender – about 30 minutes.

■ Season lightly with the salt. (Remember that with the bacon, you will need little.)

CHEF'S ASIDE

This is a dish that is remarkably easy to spoil. The whole point of it is that the chicken cooks in its own juices, flavored simply by the peppers. No onions. No other broth. The bacon on top provides the lubrication required. Splendid.

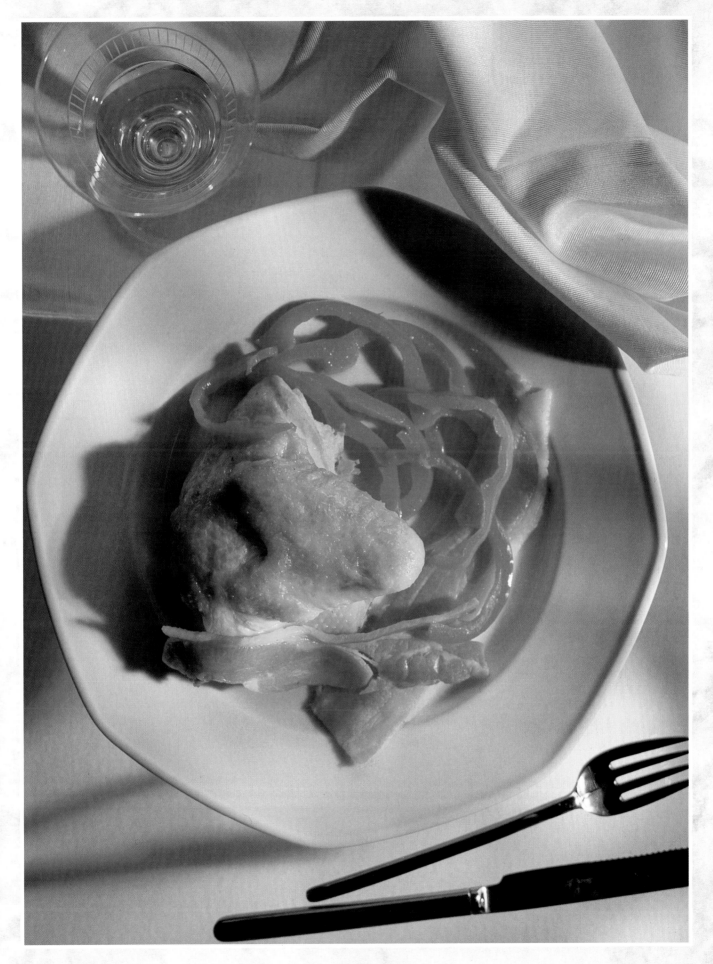

Papardelle Noodles with Tomato Sauce and Hare

PAPARDELLE AL SUGO DI LEPRE

INGREDIENTS

1 pt broth made from the bones, kidneys, and heart of a hare (*see* Pastine in Brodo, but substitute hare bones)

1¼ cups / ½ pt tomato sauce (*as for* Spaghetti al Morgan but without the fried eggplant)

½ lb papardelle noodles

1 hare liver

PREPARATION

■ *Combine the broth and the tomato sauce. Reduce both until the volume is halved.*
■ *Prepare the pasta in the usual manner (see Pasta).*
■ *Immediately before serving, mash the hare liver very finely and stir it into the very hot pasta sauce. A rich and succulent dish.*

CHEF'S TIP

This dish properly belongs in the Pasta section. However, I could not bring myself to write under ingredients, anything quite so bizarre as 'the bones, liver, kidneys, and heart of a fresh hare'. These are not items you can go out and buy. You rather acquire the animal itself and then find yourself stuck with them. But you will not be stuck. This dish of Papardelle – broad, thin noodles up to ¾ in wide – is a Piedmontese specialty and delicious.

Rolled and Pot-Roast Hare

LEPRE AL ROTOLO

SERVES 6 – 7
Preparation time 2 hours
Oven temperature 350°F

INGREDIENTS
1 large hare
½ lb unsmoked bacon or *pancetta*, the fattier the better
2 cloves garlic
1 heaping tbsp crushed fresh rosemary (half the quantity, if using dried)
1 heaping tbsp crushed fresh thyme (half the quantity, if using dried)
1 heaping tbsp crumbled fresh sage (half the quantity, if using dried)
4 tbsp olive oil
Juice of 1 lemon
½ lb *tritto* (see Tritto, p13)
½ lb fresh or canned plum tomatoes
1¼ cups / ½ pt dry white wine
Salt and freshly ground pepper to taste

PREPARATION

■ *Preheat the oven. Remove the hare's legs. Cut through the meat along the line of the bones and remove the bones. Set them aside. Batten each of the legs into an escalope about 1 cm / ⅓ in thick, (see Battening Meat Italian-style, p15).*

■ *When all four leg escalopes are nicely flat, arrange them together with their adjoining edges overlapping slightly, so they form a rough rectangle. (Just to keep you in the picture, you are going to lay strips of meat along the longer edge of this rectangle and then roll the thing up, jelly-roll-style.)*

■ *Now for the strips of meat. Running along the back of the hare – the saddle – are two thin, round strips of meat (the sirloins) and they stretch from the shoulder blades to the haunch. Run the point of a sharp knife along the top of the saddle, very close to the spine, from front to rear. This will free one sirloin from the back. Push/roll the meat down over the ribs. Cut it free as soon as there is no more meat between the skin and ribs. Pull or cut off the skin and set aside.*

■ *Lay the first sirloin along the rectangle of escalopes. Do the same with the other sirloin. Lay the bacon in long strips around the sirloins.*

■ *Cut free the fillets (the tiny triangular strips of meat on the inner side of the ribs towards the haunch and slot them into the meat strips wherever they will fit.)*

■ *Roughly crush the garlic and all the herb, and rub them into the leg meat and sirloins. Pour over half the olive oil and the lemon juice, and complete the filling with half the tritto.*

■ *Roll up the outer leg meat so the whole hare now resembles a fat and untidy sausage. Secure it with loops of string.*

■ *In as tight-fitting a casserole dish as you can find, brown the tritto in the remaining oil. Add the hare sausage and brown it evenly. Roughly chop the tomatoes and add them and the wine to the dish.*

■ *Cover and bake in the oven for about 1½ hours, or until the hare is very tender.*

■ *Season the pan juices, carve the roulade, and serve the juices spooned over it. You will have first thoughtfully removed all trace of string.*

Rabbit with Onions

CONIGLIO ARROSTO CON CIPOLLE

SERVES 4

Cooking time 1½ hours

Oven temperature
350°F

INGREDIENTS

1 large rabbit (weighing
about 2 lb)

4 tbsp olive oil

3 large onions

6 cloves garlic

6 bay leaves

3 chile peppers

4 good sprigs fresh rosemary

4 tbsp brandy

Salt and freshly grated black
pepper to taste

PREPARATION

■ *Preheat the oven. Cut away the legs from the rabbit carcass and joint each one once more at the knee. Cut the saddle into 4 pieces: haunch, belly, and the rib cage, split in two along the breast bone.*

■ *Heat the oil over a medium heat and brown the rabbit pieces for 3–4 minutes. Remove them with a slotted, spoon and set aside.*

■ *Slice the onions very fine and add them to the rabbit pan. Increase the heat and cook them until they begin to color. Reduce the heat and add the whole garlic, the whole chiles, and the whole sprigs of rosemary.*

■ *Return the rabbit to the pan and smother with the onions. Cover tightly and begin baking.*

■ *After about 1 hour, completely turn all the contents, add the brandy, and season. Continue cooking until the rabbit is very tender – another 30 minutes or so.*

CHEF'S ASIDE

How versatile is the rabbit! A cuddly, trouble-free household pet that will eat practically anything you give it, bar your fingers. And notwithstanding, a source of delight and simple pleasure to gastronomes the world over. Would we could say the same about cats.

Roast Rabbit with Lamb

CONIGLIO ARROSTO CON AGNELLO

SERVES 8 – 10

Preparation time 2 hours

Oven temperature
350°F

INGREDIENTS

1 large lamb shoulder (weighing
about 4½ lb), cut
into 8 large bone-in chunks

1 large rabbit, jointed into 8 – 4
legs, with the saddle cut into 4
pieces

1 large onion, sliced

4 cloves garlic, roughly minced

4 good sprigs rosemary

12 fresh sage leaves

1¼ cups / ½ pt dry white wine

4 tbsp dry Marsala

Salt and freshly ground black
pepper to taste

PREPARATION

■ *Preheat the oven. Heat a roasting pan to very hot. Add no oil. (There's none in the recipe, so you can't!) Drop in the lamb shoulder. Seal the lamb pieces by sautéeing very fiercely, then lower the heat until a little of the lamb fat begins to run. Remove the lamb and set aside.*

■ *Add the jointed rabbit. Seal the rabbit gently for 2–3 minutes. Remove and set aside.*

■ *Scorch the onion in what should be a very lightly greased roasting pan. Add the, garlic, rosemary, sage, and the wines. Bring everything to a boil.*

■ *Replace the meat, making sure the pieces alternate with each other: the fat of the lamb must moisten the rabbit during the cooking process and the flavor of the rabbit must permeate the lamb. Season at this point.*

■ *Cover and bake in the oven for about 1½ hours.*

CHEF'S ASIDE

This reasonably cunning combination links two meats with very different, but highly complementary, basic qualities. The result is extremely interesting. You could just squeeze by with half a shoulder and half a rabbit if you want to cook for a smaller number but, really, bulk is best: the juices flow faster and stronger.

Pigeon Breasts with Pine Nuts and Lemon

PETTI DI PICCIONCINI AL LIMONE E NOCCE DI PINI

SERVES 4
Preparation time 45 minutes
INGREDIENTS
6 young pigeons
1/3 cup / 3 fl oz *tritto* (see Tritto)
2 oz pine nuts
4 tbsp olive oil
Juice and zest of 1 lemon
2/3 cup / 1/4 pt Marsala wine

PREPARATION

▪ *Remove the breasts from the pigeons. Keeping the blade very close to the high-ridged breast bone, a swift stroke of the knife from back to front will have the breast hanging on by skin only. Cut through the skin.*

▪ *Brown the tritto in a very large pan. Roughly chop the carcasses. As the tritto browns, add them, cover with water, and bring to a boil. Allow to simmer.*

▪ *In a skillet containing no oil, toast the pine nuts until they begin to brown. Remove them from the heat immediately – they will continue to cook a little of their own accord.*

▪ *Heat the olive oil in a heavy pan and drop in each pigeon breast. Cook for no more than 10 seconds on each side. The breasts will puff up. Remove the skin then slice each breast through across the horizontal flat plane. Seal the raw sides of each breast for a further 2 – 3 seconds in the hot oil.*

▪ *Pour away most of the oil and return the pan to a high heat. Add the lemon juice, zest, and the Marsala and reduce until you have a thick syrup about 5 minutes. Stir in 2/3 cup / 1/4 pt of pigeon broth made from the carcasses and reduce again.*

▪ *Toss the breasts into the sauce and reheat for half a minute. Remove the breasts from the pan, pour the sauce over them, and sprinkle the browned pine nuts on top.*

CHEF'S TIPS

The pigeon breasts take no time at all to cook. Very hard and very fast is the golden rule here. They will be excessively tender. This recipe also wins you some extra pigeon broth, with which you can, if you wish, make a pasta sauce much along the lines of Papardelle al Sugo di Lepre, p98. Of course the smaller pigeons yield rather less broth.

Pheasant Braised with Three Alcohols

FAGIANO BRASOTO AI TRE VINI

SERVES 4

Preparation time 2½ hours

Oven temperature
325°F

INGREDIENTS

2 pheasants

4 tbsp olive oil

1 medium onion, sliced fine

2 cloves garlic

8 sprigs fresh rosemary

4 tbsp Marsala

4 tbsp brandy

⅔ cup / ¼ pt dry white wine

Salt and freshly ground black
pepper to taste

PREPARATION

■ Preheat the oven. Cut away the backbones, then slice each bird into two: cut down through the center of the breastbone.

■ In a tray large enough to hold the halves side by side, heat the oil. Soften in it the finely sliced onion. Throw the garlic in whole.

■ As the onion cooks, flatten out the pheasants as much as you can. Either press quietly and discreetly with the palm of your hand or work them over brutally with the flat of the cleaver. The latter is more fun, especially in a top floor apartment.

■ Lay the sprigs of rosemary on top of the softened onions, then lay the pheasant breasts down on top of that. Cook thus for 2 – 3 minutes on a high heat.

■ Take a fork and liberally prick the upper and stil uncooked sides of the birds. Mix the Marsala and brandy together and pour an equal amount over each bird.

■ Cover the dish very tightly and commit to the oven.

■ After 1½ hours' cooking, turn the birds, scooping all the onion and rosemary you can onto the tops of the breasts. Now add the white wine.

■ Return once more to the oven and continue cooking until the pheasants are very tender – about 1 hour more.

■ Season the pan juices at the last minute and pour on top of the birds.

CHEF'S TIP

The dish in which you cook these birds should be a perfect fit for them. If it is a little large, check the liquid levels a couple of times and moisten if necessary. A second possibilty in the case of an oversize dish is to drape ½ lb bacon over the birds.

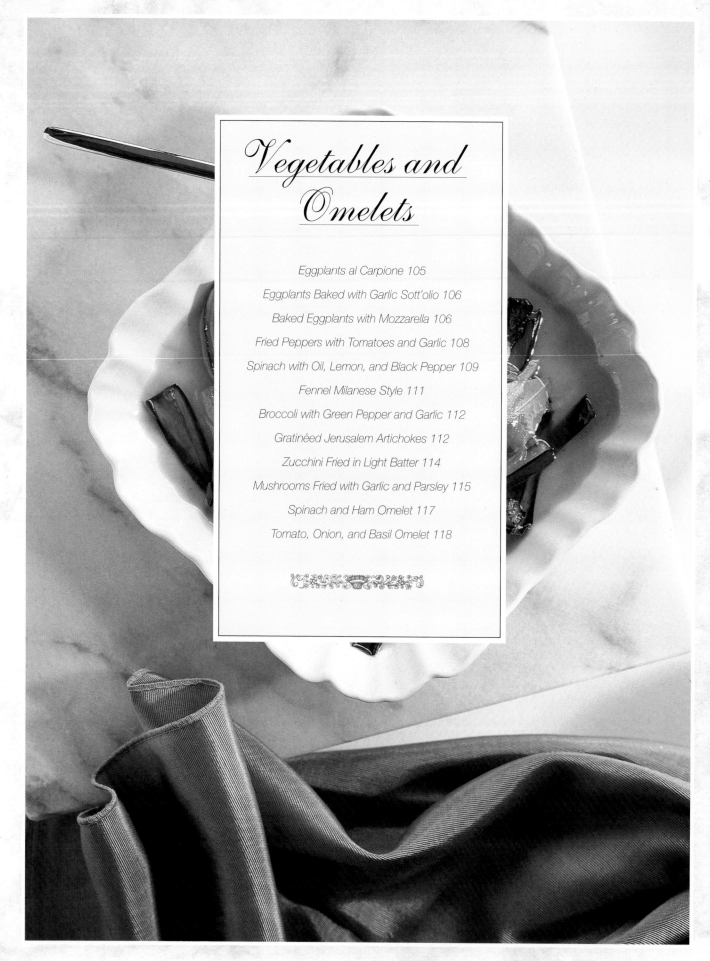

Vegetables and Omelets

Eggplants Al Carpione

MELANZANE FRITTE AL CARPIONE

SERVES 4

Preparation time 20 minutes

INGREDIENTS

1¼ cups / ½ pt olive oil

1 large onion

4 cloves garlic

⅔ cup / ¼ pt dry white wine

4 tbsp vinegar

2 tbsp sugar

2 large sprigs fresh rosemary

4 fresh bay leaves

1 chile pepper

2 medium eggplants

Salt to taste

PREPARATION

■ *Put half the olive oil in a pan and set it over medium heat.*

■ *Slice the onion very fine and stew it in the oil. (Stew, not fry.) Add the garlic and cook both together until the onion is soft. It must not color.*

■ *Add the wine, vinegar, sugar, rosemary, bay leaves, and the whole chile. Bring the mixture to a boil, then remove it from the heat and season it. Reserve.*

■ *Cut the eggplants into 1½-in batons and fry them in batches in the remaining oil over a high-ish heat. Cook them until they wrinkle and brown severely.*

■ *Set each batch to drain on paper towels as you undertake the next.*

■ *When all eggplant is cooked, arrange it in a dish.*

■ *Simply pour the wine and oil mixture over it, stand back, and marvel.*

CHEF'S ASIDE

This dish, with the wizened chocolate color of the fried eggplants covered by the slender, pale strands of onion, whole clumps of rosemary, dangerous looking pieces of garlic, and the sheen of the oil and wine, looks utterly magnificent. It tastes even better.

Eggplants Baked with Garlic Sott'olio

MELANZANE AL FORNO SOTT'OLIO

SERVES 4 – 6

Preparation time
15 minutes

Oven temperature 400°F

INGREDIENTS

2 large eggplants

4 cloves garlic

²⁄₃ cup / ¼ pt olive oil

Juice of half a lemon

Salt and freshly ground black pepper

PREPARATION

■ Preheat the oven. Cut the spiky stalk from the eggplants. Peel the garlic cloves and cut them lengthwise into thinnish slivers.

■ Pierce the eggplants all over with a thin bladed knife. Push the slivers of garlic into the slits.

■ Place the eggplants directly onto the wire shelving of the oven. Do not oil them in any way. Bake for 15 minutes, until the vegetables shrink into themselves and the skins wrinkle. When cooked, they will feel soft to the touch.

■ Remove the eggplant from the oven and allow them to stand for 3–4 minutes.

■ Slice them into neat, thin, strips lengthwise. Dress them with the oil, lemon juice, salt, and pepper.

■ Serve hot, warm or cool.

CHEF'S ASIDE

The simplest is the best. Cooked in this way, the eggplants steam in their own juices, hermetically sealed by their skins. The flavored steam also picks up the scent of the garlic and forces it through the plant. Magnificent. Another lovely dressing would be *Aglio olio e peperoncini* (see Insalata di Calamaretti, and Spaghetti Aglio, Olio e Peperroncini).

Baked Eggplants with Mozzarella

MELANZANE ALLA PARMIGIANA

SERVES 4

Preparation time about
30 minutes

Oven temperature
400°F

INGREDIENTS

2 medium eggplants

4 tbsp olive oil

1 lb fresh or canned plum tomatoes

2 tbsp fresh oregano (half the quantity for dried)

Salt and freshly ground black pepper

½ lb Mozzarella cheese

3 tbsp freshly grated Parmesan cheese

PREPARATION

■ Preheat the oven. Cut off the coarse stalks of the eggplants and slice them lengthwise in ½-in slices. Bake the slices in the oven, directly on the wire shelving, for 10 minutes or until very soft.

■ In the meantime, oil a baking dish. Chop the tomatoes roughly and combine with the oregano. Season strongly with the salt and pepper. Grate the Mozzarella and mix it with the Parmesan.

■ Remove the eggplant slices from the oven and line the baking dish with one layer. Spread the tomato and oregano mixture evenly over it, and sprinkle the Mozzarella and Parmesan on top of that. Continue these layers until the dish is full, leaving yourself a good amount of Mozzarella and Parmesan as a final, thick coating: the cheese will melt and seal the dish as it cooks.

■ Bake until the cheese melts and browns – 15–20 minutes.

Fried Peppers with Tomato and Garlic
PEPERONATA

SERVES 4
Cooking time 20 minutes
INGREDIENTS
6 medium bell peppers, 3 red and 3 green
4 tbsp olive oil
3 cloves garlic, minced
6 oz fresh or canned plum tomatoes
Salt to taste

PREPARATION

■ Halve and deseed the peppers and slice crosswise into ¼-in strips.

■ Heat the oil in a shallow pan large enough to hold all the peppers comfortably. Add the peppers and the minced garlic cloves. Cook over medium heat until the peppers begin to soften.

■ As the peppers cook, roughly chop the tomatoes. If they are fresh, skin them. Add the tomatoes to the peppers in the pan, cover, and reduce the heat to simmer.

■ Season when the peppers have softened completely – about 15 minutes. Serve hot, warm, or cold.

Spinach with Oil, Lemon, and Black Pepper

SPINACI CONDITI

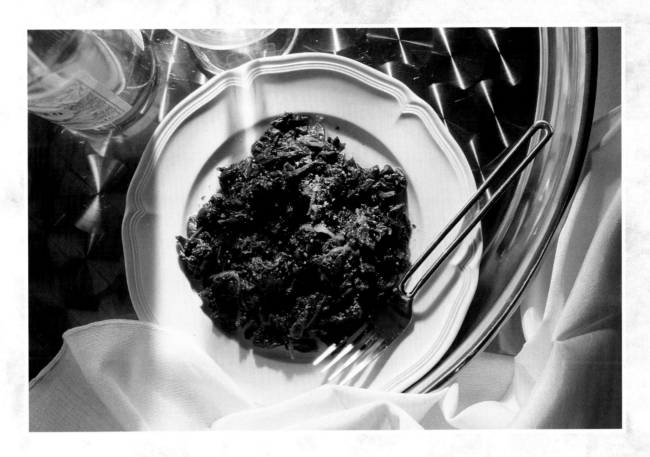

SERVES 4 – 6
Cooking time 15 minutes
INGREDIENTS
2 lb fresh spinach
⅔ cup / ¼ pt olive oil
Juice of half a lemon
Salt and a copious quantity of freshly ground black pepper

PREPARATION

▪ *Trim the stalks from the spinach leaves (see Chef's Tips).*

▪ *Very lightly oil the bottom of a thick pan and set it on a low heat. Introduce the spinach a little at a time. It will shrink as it comes in contact with the heat. Cover the pan and steam the spinach for about 10 minutes over a fairly low heat.*

▪ *When the spinach is cooked, press it lightly in a colander and secure the juices for another use (see Chef's Tip's). Allow the spinach to cool slightly. Then simply dress it with the olive oil, lemon juice, salt, and pepper.*

▪ *Eat it hot, warm, or cool.*

CHEF'S TIPS

You can make soup with the spinach stalks, as you can with the juices of the spinach, if you go to the trouble of keeping it for later use, either in the refrigerator or in the freezer.

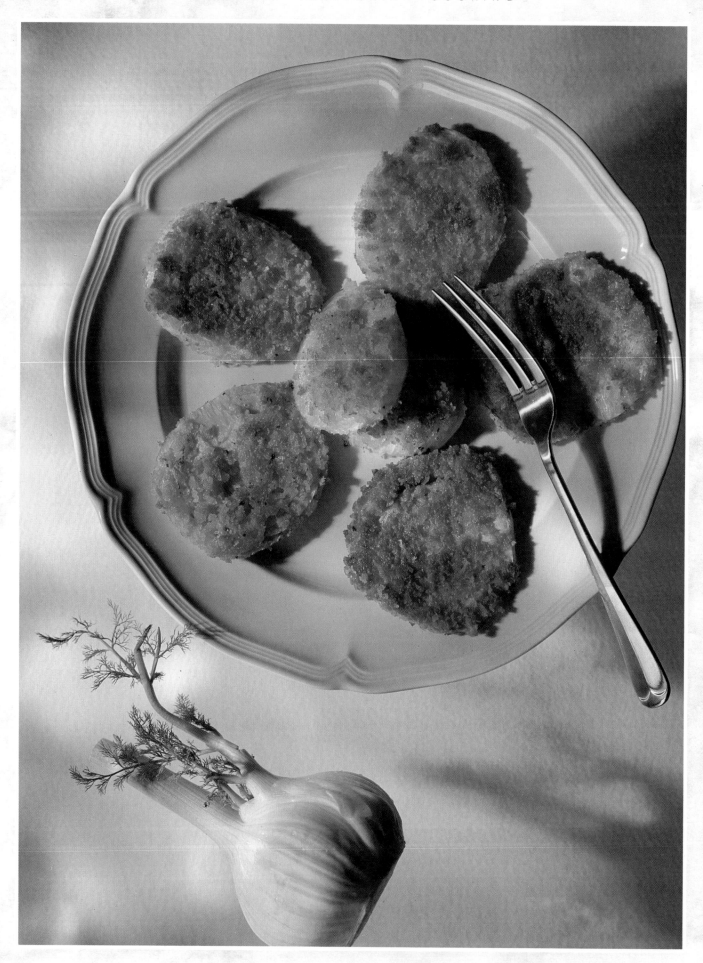

Fennel Milanese Style
FINOCCHIO MILANESE

SERVERS 4 – 6

Preparation time 25 minutes

INGREDIENTS

3 medium fennel bulbs

⅔ cup / ¼ pt white wine

2 tbsp vinegar

1 clove garlic

2 bay leaves

Salt to taste

2 eggs

3 cups fresh bread crumbs

⅔ cup / ¼ pt olive oil

PREPARATION

■ The fennel, though bulb-like, is also slightly flattened. So cut it into ¼-in slices from the root upwards, in the same plane as its flat side. You will find that the inner 3 or 4 slices hang together as cross-sections of the plant. Set all these aside.

■ Put the rest, with the white wine, vinegar, garlic, and bay leaves, into 4 cups / 2 pt water, and bring everything to a boil. Salt the liquid to taste and poach the fennel cross sections in it for 10 – 15 minutes or until soft (see Chef's Tips). Drain the fennel and pat it dry.

■ In a shallow bowl, beat the two eggs well. Dip each fennel piece into the egg, covering it well. Shake off any excess. Now press the fennel slices forcefully into the bread crumbs, spread out on an open surface to facilitate the process.

■ Heat the oil to a fast-frying temperature; fry each fennel slice until crisp on both sides. Eat hot.

CHEF'S TIPS

Poaching liquids like this can often come in handy. There is no reason, therefore, why you should not strain them after use and keep them chilled or frozen. Incidentally, if you are going to ask about this dish in Italy, watch how you go about it. *Finocchio* is also Italian slang for homosexual! Pronunciation note: the word is pronounced "fin-ock:ee-o!". You will see that "cch" comes out as an English "k" (So does "ch", as it happens.) Now for the exam, how do you pronounce "radicchio"? (*see* Zuppa di Radicchio con Salvia.)

111

Broccoli with Green Pepper and Garlic

BROCCOLI ALL' AGLIO E PEPERONI VERDI

SERVES 4 – 6

Preparation 6 – 8 minutes

INGREDIENTS

1½ lb fresh broccoli

Salt to taste

5 tsp olive oil

1 small green bell pepper, deseeded and sliced fine

4 cloves garlic

¾ tbsp freshly grated Parmesan cheese

Freshly grated black pepper

PREPARATION

▮ Bring plenty of salted water to the boil, drop in the trimmed broccoli florets, and boil for 3 minutes. Drain them and stop the cooking process by plunging them in cold water.

▮ Heat the olive oil over a high heat. Cook the pepper in the oil until the slices begin to brown slightly at the edges. Reduce the heat and add the garlic cloves, well minced. Cook the pepper and garlic together for 1 – 2 minutes.

▮ Add the broccoli and the Parmesan, and turn in the oil and Parmesan until the broccoli is hot.

▮ Serve immediately, lavishly sprinkled with the pepper.

CHEF'S TIP

The Parmesan is as much for grain as for taste – hence the small quantity.

Gratinéed Jerusalem Artichokes

TOPINAMBURI GRATINATI

SERVES 4 – 6

Preparation time 15 – 20 minutes

Oven temperature 400°F

INGREDIENTS

1 lb Jerusalem artichokes (see Chef's Tips)

Salt

4 tbsp butter

3 tbsp freshly grated Parmesan cheese

Freshly grated black pepper

PREPARATION

▮ Preheat the oven. Scrub the artichokes in a robust fashion and cut away any darker patches of skin. (There is no need to peel them, unless you have all week.)

▮ Drop the artichokes in boiling salted water – cover well – and cook for 10 minutes. They should be firm but easily biteable. Remove them from their cauldron, drain, and slice thinly.

▮ Grease a baking dish with a little of the butter and layer it with the artichokes. Dot the rest of the butter over the top.

▮ Sprinkle with the Parmesan and a stiff measure of pepper. Bake them until the cheese and butter form an enticing brown crust. Serve very hot.

CHEF'S TIPS

These artichokes are, as you probably know, nothing to do with the other sort. On a further point of information, they resemble heavily mis-shapen potatoes or fresh ginger root. Their unique and delectable flavor makes splendid soups, especially when puréed with chicken broth.

Zucchini Fried in Light Batter

ZUCCHINI FRITTI CON LA PASTELLA

SERVES 4
Cooking time 6 – 10 minutes

INGREDIENTS
1 lb zucchini
1 cup all-purpose flour
Salt and pepper to taste
1¼ cups / ½ pt vegetable oil

PREPARATION

■ Slice the zucchini into batons approximately ½ in thick and 2 in long, depending on the size of the individual vegetables.

■ Sift the flour with the salt and pepper, then mix it very gradually with water, beating constantly to avoid lumps. Stop when your batter is the consistency of thick cream.

■ Heat the oil until very hot, dip the zucchini in the batter, and then fry in batches – they should fit only loosely into the pan. When the batter is crisp and brown, the vegetables are ready.

■ Like all fried food, they should be served very hot.

CHEF'S TIP

It is sometimes difficult to recommend quantities of oil in cases like this. Since this recipe requires deep frying, the depth, with a fixed volume of oil, will clearly vary with the diameter of the pan. Bear in mind that there should be enough oil for the sliced zucchini to float.

Mushrooms Fried with Garlic and Parsley

FUNGHI TRIFOLATI

SERVES 6
Cooking time about 5 minutes

INGREDIENTS

1½ lb good mushrooms
(see Chef's Tips)

4 tbsp olive oil

3 cloves garlic, minced

2 heaping tbsp chopped
fresh parsley

Salt and freshly ground black
pepper to taste

PREPARATION

■ Wash but do not peel – never peel – the mushrooms. Slice or chop them into thumb-size chunks if they are particularly large.

■ Heat the oil to medium and sauté the minced garlic for 30 seconds or so. Add the mushrooms. These will absorb the oil very promptly. When they do, turn down the heat and wait for the process to reverse – the mushrooms begin to give off their own liquor. This will take 2 minutes or so.

■ Increase the heat and add the parsley, salt, and pepper. Cook for a further 2–3 minutes and serve.

CHEF'S TIPS

The Italian verb 'to fry with garlic and parsley' is *trifolare* and you will find quite a number of things *trifolati* – zucchini for example.

And what is a good mushroom? What is *not* a good mushroom is that small, white, perfectly symmetrical item that looks like a children's storybook illustration.

Spinach and Ham Omelet

FRITTATA DI SPINACI E PROSCIUTTO

Before we get down to business here, a word about the Italian omelet. It is not the light and runny affair of France but a thick, multi-egged and completely cooked number, served in wedges like a cake, often cold. Such dishes may be eaten at the evening meal, which in Italy is traditionally much lighter than lunch.

SERVES 4
Preparation time 20 minutes
INGREDIENTS
6 eggs
3 tbsp freshly grated Parmesan cheese
4 oz Parma ham, roughly chopped
6 oz cooked spinach (*see* Spinaci Conditi)
Salt and pepper to taste
4 tbsp olive oil

PREPARATION

■ *Thoroughly beat the eggs. Mix in the cheese, ham, spinach, salt, and pepper.*
■ *Heat the oil over a medium heat, in as heavy a pan as you have. Pour in the mixture and then turn the heat down as low as it will go. Cover the pan and cook until everything is set – about 20 minutes.*
■ *Serve at whatever temperature you wish.*

Tomato, Onion, and Basil Omelet

FRITTATA CON POMODORI CIPOLLE E BASILICO

SERVES 4
Preparation time 30 minutes
INGREDIENTS
4 tbsp olive oil
1 medium onion, chopped fine
½ lb fresh or canned plum tomatoes
3 tbsp roughly chopped fresh basil
6 eggs
3 tbsp freshly grated Parmesan cheese
Salt and pepper to taste

PREPARATION

■ *Heat a little over half the oil in a heavy pan. Add the onions and cook until soft – about 3 – 4 minutes.*

■ *As the onions are cooking, roughly chop the tomatoes. Add them when the onions are ready. Turn up the heat and reduce the pan liquids by a good third.*

■ *Toss in the roughly chopped basil and remove the pan from the heat.*

■ *In a bowl, beat the eggs thoroughly. Add the cheese, fold the tomato mixture into the eggs, and season well. Replace the pan on the heat, and pour in the remaining oil. Scrape the egg and tomato mixture into the pan, turn the heat down very low, and cover. Cook until everything is set, about 20 minutes.*

■ *Serve at any temperature but chilled.*

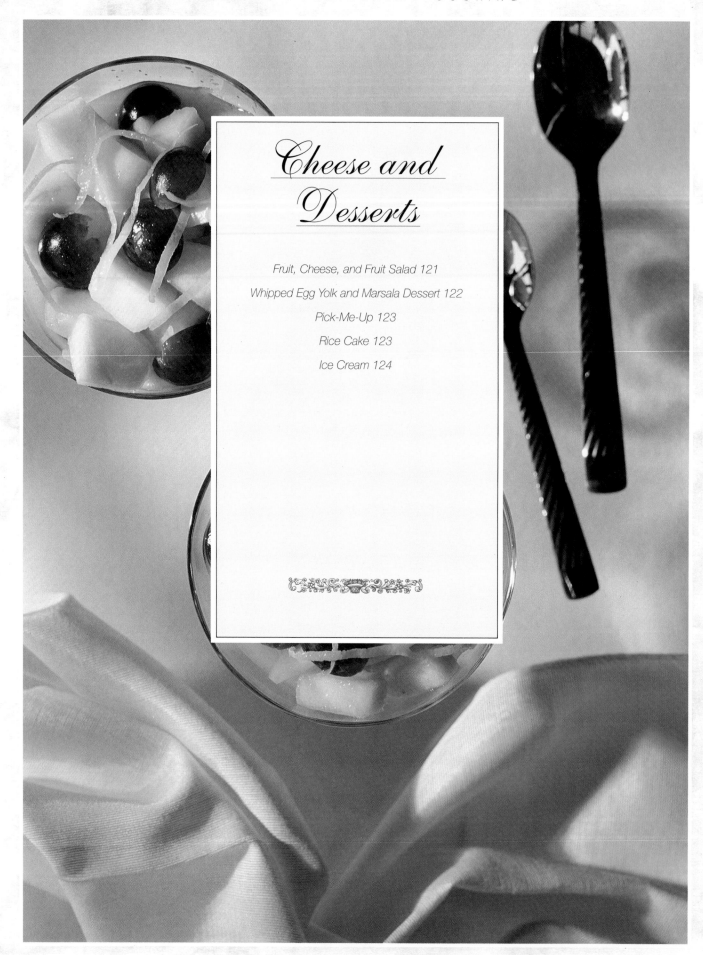

Cheese and Desserts

Fruit, Cheese, and Fruit Salad

FRUTTA, FORMAGGIO E MACEDONIA DI FRUTTA

A word or two in your ear about desserts and the Italian meal. The two do not really go together. When some breathtakingly elegant *antipasto* of, let us say, tiny artichokes eaten whole with lemon juice, oil, and black pepper has been consumed, followed by the Stygian perfume of Risotto Nero alle Seppie, a perfect slice of roast veal, its thin, rosemary-scented gravy, and the concentrated summer richness of Melanzane al Forno spicily dressed with chile and garlic, the discriminating Italian diner is in no mood for Black Forest torte or apple pie, even if it is written in French. Simple ice cream seems too contrived a choice. No. What the discriminating Italian diner desires is the rude perfection of excellent cheese and the season's fruit at its peak.

Like what? Well, a chunk of fresh, moist Parmesan is always superb. As is Pecorino, either the sweet, dolce kind or the hard, spicy one. Fontina and Taleggio are magnificent with firm pears. Dolcelatte and Gorgonzola should be eaten with very fresh Italian bread, on which, with these cheeses, the Italians sometimes scrape a little butter – very unusual. And as for the sight of those huge, lightly chilled peaches glowing in the bowl at your elbow, it's like that feeling you got in the old days when you knew the insurance would always pay up.

I have given some dessert recipes, of course, and I shall begin with the simplest. Macedonia di Frutta, Italian Fruit Salad.

Italian Fruit Salad

MACEDONIA DI FRUTTA

SERVES ABOUT 6

Preparation time 10 minutes

Marinating time at least 4 hours

INGREDIENTS

1¼ cups / ½ pt fresh orange juice

Zest and juice of one lemon

2 apples

2 firm pears

2 firm bananas

1½ lb assorted fruit, such as peaches, apricots, melon, grapes, cherries, mangoes

4 tbsp white sugar

4 tbsp Grappa or Grand Marnier

PREPARATION

■ *Mix the orange juice, lemon juice, and zest.*
■ *Peel all the fruit except for the grapes and cherries. Deseed everything. As each fruit is peeled, chop it to grape size and add it to the fruit juice mixture immediately to stop it discoloring in the air.*
■ *Sprinkle the the sugar over, pour on the liqueur, and chill for at least 4 hours if you can. Stir the mixture – carefully – 2 or 3 times during the chilling process.*

Whipped Egg Yolk and Marsala Dessert

ZABAGLIONE

SERVES 6

Preparation time 10 – 15 minutes

INGREDIENTS

6 eggs

¾ cup confectioners' sugar

6 tbsp Marsala wine

PREPARATION

■ Separate the eggs and yolk. Beat the yolks with the sugar and the wine.

■ Place the bowl containing the egg mixture into the saucepan filled with hot water, or pour into the egg mixture into top part of the double broiler.

■ Begin to beat the egg mixture – a fork will not be good enough. Minimum for manual operation is a good, bendy whisk. Ideal is a hand-held electrical version. As the air is incorporated into the eggs, it will swell from the heat of the water. It will also stiffen as the heat of the water cooks it.

■ Whisk until the mixture increases its volume by at least 3 times and stiffens until it is only just pourable.

■ Decant into fine, fluted glasses. The perfect example would be Venetian in manufacture and Baroque in conception. Eat with spoons and those little biscuits the Italians called amaretti.

CHEF'S ASIDE

With a very good whisk, this dessert is stunningly simple. The caveat is the usual one with eggs and double broilers: don't let the water boil and overcook the eggs. You can control the process quite finely by lifting the pan in and out of the water bath.

Here are some unorthodox variations:

■ Add the zest of an orange to the egg mixture before cooking.

■ Add a thumb-size lump of candied ginger sliced very very fine.

■ Use port Instead of Marsala.

■ Zabaglione can also be a rather classy substitute for cream. With strawberries, for example.

Pick-Me-Up
TIRAMISU

SERVES 8
Preparation time 2 – 3 hours
INGREDIENTS
4 eggs
4 tbsp Marsala Wine
¾ cup confectioners' sugar
½ lb Mascarpone (or cottage cheese)
1¼ cups / ½ pt strong coffee, sweetened with 2 oz white sugar
40 ladyfingers (about 1 in each)
4 oz dark chocolate

PREPARATION

■ *Separate the eggs and the yolks. Set aside 2 whites in another bowl.*

■ *Combine the yolks, the wine, and the sugar and beat together.*

■ *Bring a pan of water to just below boiling, then turn down to simmer and beat the yolk mixture over the water until it begins to swell and thicken. (Use a double boiler or saucepan, if you have one.) Set the yolks aside.*

■ *Whisk the two remaining whites into stiff peaks and fold them into the yolk mixture, then set aside.*

■ *Liquidize the cheese in a processor or blender and fold into it the yolk and white mixture. Check the sweetness at this stage and adjust it to taste.*

■ *Dip each ladyfinger in the coffee: let it soak well. Arrange a floor of ladyfingers on your dish, then spread them with a thin coating of the egg/cheese mixture. Repeat the process until you have used your last layer of egg/cheese.*

■ *Run a knife around the edges of your little building to smooth down the sides. Grate the chocolate and sprinkle it over sides and top. Chill until completely cold and set.*

Rice Cake
TORTA DI RISO

SERVES ABOUT 6
Preparation time 4 hours
Standing time 24 hours
Oven temperature 350°F
INGREDIENTS
4 cups / 1½ pt milk
Pinch of salt
2 cups white sugar
Zest of 1 lemon
⅓ cup risotto rice
5 yolks and four whites of eggs
2 oz almonds
2 oz pine nuts
2 oz candied peel
4 tbsp Grappa
4 tbsp butter, melted

PREPARATION

■ *Preheat the oven. Bring milk, salt, sugar, and lemon to a boil on top of the stove, and add the rice.*

■ *Cook until the rice is completely dissolved. The mixture should have the dense consistency of porridge. Remove it from the heat and let it cool.*

■ *Beat the eggs until well amalgamated.*

■ *Lightly toast the almonds and pine nuts – but remember, they toast very quickly so do not burn them.*

■ *Stir the toasted nuts, the candied peel, and the Grappa into the rice mixture, then beat it slowly into the eggs.*

■ *Liberally grease with the butter a cake pan large enough to hold all the mixure. Pour it all in.*

■ *Bake for about 1 hour, or until the proverbial knife, inserted in the center comes out as it went in. Let the cake cool until it is easy to handle, but still warm, and then ease it from its container.*

■ *Let it stand, if possible for 24 hours, before serving. It will go on improving for a week or so after that.*

Ice Cream

GELATO

SERVES 4
Preparation time about 4 hours maximum

INGREDIENTS
2½ cups / 1 pt milk
2 vanilla beans
Zest of half a lemon
½ cup white sugar
6 eggs

PREPARATION

■ Bring the milk to a boil in a saucepan with the vanilla beans, lemon zest, and half the sugar. Remove from the heat and let it stand.

■ Now separate the egg yolks from the whites and beat the yolks with the sugar.

■ Over a double boiler (see instructions for Zabaglione, p121) beat the egg yolks until they begin to foam and the volume begins to increase. Remove from the heat and slowly beat in the milk.

■ Return to the heat and cook slowly for five minutes or so, until you have a liquid the consistency of thick cream. Then pour the mixture directly into the bowl of your ice cream machine and switch on, or let the mixture cool to barely lukewarm and freeze. (With the second method, you must beat the mixture well once it has frozen to a slush. This will help to break down the ice crystals, which are an almost inevitable feature of non-paddled ice cream.)

Conclusion

Italian food is widely misunderstood, a problem for which Italian restaurants outside Italy must share a good deal of the blame. What I have to do with the limited number of recipes in this book is to redress the imbalance a little. That is why there are only two dishes involving cream and no recipe for Bolognese sauce. My ability to attempt this feat is thanks principally to two pleople: Olga Bernardi of Capanna Kind, a restaurant with rooms near Salice D'Ulzio in the Piedmontese Alps, and her sometime chef Giorgio Raisa from the Veneto, now fortunately both a friend and colleague of mine. So cheers to both of you, once again.

I have a feeling, however, that Italian cooking will not remain off the map for long. Things are stirring here, mark my words.

Lastly, the problem of recipes in general. They are compiled with the benefit of hindsight, except in certain cases where some fanatic deliberately tries to create a new dish on paper before cooking it. (It can be done!) It pretty well follows, however, that the recipe is not a tramline. All it does is describe a sequence of events which happened to a certain extent by chance. Always remember this. It will free you from the tyranny of cook books, whose proper place is not in the kitchen but in an armchair by the fireside.

Index